AS Sociology

Contents

Introduction

■ ■ ■

Content Guidance

■ ■ ■

Questions and Answers

Introduction

About this guide

This unit guide is for students following the OCR AS Sociology course. It deals with the Module 2532 topic **The Individual and Society**. This topic is designed to give you a basic introduction to sociological theories aimed at understanding human behaviour. It focuses on how culture is formed, the role of primary and secondary agents of socialisation and identity formation in relation to gender, ethnicity, nationality and social class.

There are three sections to this guide:

- **Introduction** — this provides advice on how to use this unit guide, an explanation of the skills required in AS Sociology and suggestions for effective revision. It concludes with guidance on how to succeed in the unit test.
- **Content Guidance** — this provides an outline of what is included in the specification for The Individual and Society. It is designed to make you aware of what you should know before the unit test.
- **Questions and Answers** — this provides mock exam questions on The Individual and Society for you to try, together with some sample answers at grade-A and grade-C level. Examiner's comments are included on how the marks are awarded.

How to use the guide

To use this guide to your best advantage, you should refer to the Introduction and Content Guidance sections from the beginning of your study of The Individual and Society. However, in order to get full advantage from the Question and Answer section, you would be advised to wait until you have completed your study of the topic, as the questions are wide-ranging. When you are ready to use this section, you should take each question in turn, study it carefully, and either write a full answer yourself or, at the very least, answer parts (a) and (b) fully and write a plan for parts (c) and (d). When you have done this, study the grade-A candidate's answer and compare it with your own, paying close attention to the examiner's comments. You could also look at the grade-C answers and, using the examiner's comments as a guide, work out how to rewrite them to gain higher marks.

These tasks are quite intensive and time-consuming, and you are advised not to try to tackle all the questions at once or in a short space of time. It is better to focus on one at a time, and spread the workload over several weeks — you can always find some time to do this, even while studying another topic. In addition to using the questions to consolidate your own knowledge and develop your exam

27453

AS Sociology
UNIT 1

Module 2532: The Individual and Society

Steve Chapman

To the OCR AS team with thanks for all your hard work: Ann, Carole, Dave, Fionnuala and Viv

Philip Allan Updates
Market Place
Deddington
Oxfordshire
OX15 0SE

tel: 01869 338652
fax: 01869 337590
e-mail: sales@philipallan.co.uk
www.philipallan.co.uk

This Guide has been written specifically to support students preparing for the OCR AS Sociology Unit 1 examination. The content has been neither approved nor endorsed by OCR and remains the sole responsibility of the author.

Printed by Raithby, Lawrence & Co. Ltd, Leicester

skills, you should use at least some of the questions as revision practice — even just reading through the grade-A candidates' answers should provide you with useful revision material.

The AS specification

The aims of the OCR AS Sociology specification are:
- to give you a sound introduction to sociology regardless of whether you are only interested in gaining the AS award or whether you are aiming for the full A-level
- to develop in you an applied sociological knowledge and understanding of the concepts underpinning contemporary social processes and structures that are relevant to your social identity and your experiences of the social world in the twenty-first century
- to equip you with a theoretical awareness of how sociological perspectives explain the world you live in
- to examine how sociologists go about collecting information about the social world in which you live and whether their views on how your everyday world is organised are truthful and worthwhile
- to equip you with the necessary skills to engage in sociological debate, especially in terms of being able to interpret, apply and evaluate relevant evidence and to construct convincing sociological arguments
- to develop in you an appreciation and understanding that sociology is an inter-connected academic discipline that requires you to make links between different topic areas, especially with regard to inequality and difference, and the methods of sociological enquiry

Examinable skills

There are three main examinable skills in the AS specifications, divided into two **Assessment Objectives.**

Assessment Objective 1

Assessment Objective 1 (AO1) is **knowledge and understanding**, which accounts for 54% of the AS marks on offer. After studying AS Sociology, you should be able to demonstrate knowledge and understanding of sociological concepts, methods and different types of evidence, especially empirical studies. In some units, there is a need to demonstrate some introductory knowledge of theory and especially the concepts behind it. You will need to show in a clear and effective manner how concepts, evidence and methods are interlinked, and how they relate to both social life and social problems.

It is important that your acquisition of knowledge goes beyond learning by rote. You also need to demonstrate understanding. Generally this is done by learning and using knowledge that is appropriate and relevant to the question set. A good way of doing this is to ask yourself the following questions:

- Do I know the main arguments in the area I am studying?
- Do I know the main sociologists who have contributed to debate in this area?
- Do I understand the concepts used by these sociologists?
- Do I know the empirical studies and data that can be used as evidence to support or undermine particular sociological arguments?

It is important to stress here that an advanced understanding of sociological theory is not required or expected. Rather, at this level, you should be 'conceptually confident', meaning that you should be able to demonstrate that you understand important concepts and are able to apply them when constructing a sociological argument. It is also a good idea to know some sociological studies because these often count as evidence in support of a particular view.

Assessment Objective 2

Assessment Objective 2 (AO2) is broken down into **AO2(a) interpretation and analysis**, which is worth 26% of the AS marks on offer, and **AO2(b) evaluation**, which is worth 20% of the AS marks.

Interpretation and analysis essentially involves showing the ability to select and analyse different types of evidence and data. In particular, it involves the ability to apply and link sociological evidence to specific sociological arguments. It also involves the ability to interpret quantitative and qualitative data, i.e. to work out what the data are saying and/or to put them into your own words. It is useful to ask yourself the following questions when working out whether you have acquired this skill:

- What knowledge in the form of studies, concepts etc. is relevant when addressing a particular debate?
- Can I distinguish between facts and opinions?
- Am I capable of identifying patterns and trends in sociological data and uncovering hidden meanings?
- Am I addressing the question throughout the response?
- Am I using the data and information that the examiners have given to me to full effect?
- Have I applied contemporary issues and debates to the question?
- What evidence in the form of sociological studies and statistical data can I use to support or criticise particular arguments?

Evaluation normally involves assessing the validity of particular sociological arguments and available evidence and data, or critically examining the reliability of the methods used to collect that evidence. The skill of evaluation is an important one and should be applied to all the material you come across during your study of the topic. It is useful to ask yourself the following questions when practising this skill:

- How many sides to the debate can be identified in this area?
- How was the evidence gathered?
- Can the evidence be checked?
- Is there any other evidence relating to this?
- Is the research relevant to contemporary society?
- Who does not agree with this view and why?
- Which evidence and arguments are most convincing and why?
- What have they got to gain from saying that?
- Are class, gender and ethnicity taken into account?

In more practical terms, evaluation means that whenever you are introduced to a sociological perspective or study, you should find and learn at least two criticisms that have been made of it. You should also note, of course, which group or person has made these criticisms, as this is an important piece of information.

Study skills and revision strategies

Good preparation for revision actually starts the minute you begin to study sociology. One of the most important revision aids that you will have is your sociology folder, so it is important that you keep this in good order. Essentially, it should be divided into topic areas. It should contain all your class notes, handouts, notes you have made from textbooks, class and homework exercises and, of course, all your marked and returned work. If you are not by nature a neat and tidy person, you may find that you have to rewrite notes you make in class into a legible and coherent form before putting them in your folder. Be warned, though — this is something you should do straight away, as even after only a few days you will have forgotten things. If you keep a good folder throughout, reading through this will form a major part of your revision. In addition, you will, of course, need to re-read the relevant parts of your textbooks. Your own work also forms an important revision resource. Go back over your essays and exam answers, read your teacher's comments, and use these to see whether you can redo any pieces that did not score particularly good marks.

You should always write down the definition of a concept when you first come across it — it is a good idea to use a separate part of your folder for this purpose. In addition, it is useful to make a brief summary of research studies, particularly those not found in your textbook. Remember to include the title, author(s) and, most importantly, the date along with your summary of the method(s) used and the main findings. These should be kept in a section in your sociology folder, or you may wish to use a set of index cards for this purpose.

Another important aspect of revision is to practise writing answers within the appropriate time limit. Make sure you have sufficient time not only to complete all the parts of the question, but also to re-read your answer, in order to correct any silly mistakes that may have crept in while working under pressure.

Finally, you need to ensure that you have a thorough understanding of a range of appropriate concepts and studies. Again, this planned and comprehensive revision is not something that can be done the night before the exam — you should start at least a couple of weeks before the exam and revise in concentrated bursts of time. People differ in this respect, but it is seldom a good idea to spend more than 2 hours at a time on revision, and for most people, two or three stints of an hour at a time spread out over a day or two will be more productive than a 2 or 3-hour session.

The unit test

The Individual and Society is the only Module 2532 topic and the unit examination will contain a choice of two data–response questions. You will have to answer one of these in 1 hour. The unit as a whole is worth 30% of the AS marks and 15% of the full A-level. Each data–response question totals 60 marks, composed of 32 marks for AO1 (knowledge and understanding), 16 marks for AO2a (interpretation and analysis) and 12 marks for AO2b (evaluation).

Each question in the examination will contain an **item** of source material, entitled Item A for question 1 and Item B for question 2. The item is designed to assist your understanding of the area of the unit being examined and to guide you in the right direction. It is therefore essential that you spend some time carefully reading through the item. Some parts of the question, usually part (a) but also occasionally part (b), will make a specific reference to the item. Here are some types of exam command that you may encounter when being instructed to use the item for **part (a)** questions:
- 'Identify and briefly explain two social roles mentioned in Item A.'
- 'Identify and briefly explain two ways in which Item A challenges the idea of ...'
- 'Identify and briefly explain two ways in which masculine identity may be reinforced by the advertisements in Item A.'
- 'Identify and briefly explain the term "ascribed roles" using only Item A.'
- 'Using Item A, identify and briefly explain two differences between ...'

When **part (b)** questions refer to the data, they are likely to take the following form:
- 'Identify and explain two social roles, other than those mentioned in Item B.'

In all these cases you must clearly follow the instruction. It is also a good idea to make clear that you are using the item when you respond. For example, with regard to the first example listed above, you might respond, 'The two social roles mentioned in Item A are...'.

Each question is broken down into four parts, (a) to (d), each with its own mark allocation. Part (a) is worth 8 marks and focuses on the material in Item A. The item will be composed of a picture, a cartoon or a piece of text, although there is the possibility of some sort of numerical data in the form of a graph, table, pie chart etc. The marks for this question belong to AO2a (interpretation and analysis), which means the examiners are looking to see how well you have interpreted and analysed the information in the item. This question will always use the command phrase 'identify and briefly explain' and will instruct you to focus on two things related to the central concepts fundamental to this unit, e.g. 'ways' in which these concepts might do something, 'differences' between concepts, and 'features' or 'characteristics' of particular concepts. It is therefore essential when responding to this question that you clearly distinguish between two things in your identification and, moreover, that you explain their meaning, perhaps adding clarity to your explanation by using illustration and example. However, don't get carried away with your response. You should spend approximately 8 minutes on your answer and aim for two well-developed paragraphs.

The part (b) question is also worth 8 marks. The marks for this question belong to AO1 (knowledge and understanding). The question particularly aims to test your knowledge of the concepts associated with this unit, and the sociological studies and theories that can be used to illustrate your understanding of these. This question uses the command phrase 'identify and briefly explain' and will ask you to focus on two things related to the central concepts that underpin this unit, e.g. 'ways' in which these concepts might do something, 'differences' between concepts, and 'features' or 'characteristics' of particular concepts. It is therefore important again to distinguish clearly between two things in your identification and to explain their meaning using illustration and example whenever possible. Again, you should spend approximately 8 minutes on your response and aim for two well-developed paragraphs.

The part (c) question is worth 18 marks. The marks for this question are distributed across the three skills: 10 are for AO1 (knowledge and understanding), 4 are for AO2a (interpretation and analysis) and 4 are for AO2b (evaluation). This question focuses on how culture and the parts that go to make it up, i.e. values, norms, roles, statuses, etc., are transmitted, influenced and reinforced through agencies of socialisation and aspects of social life. The question will always use the command phrase 'outline and briefly evaluate' and focus on two 'ways' in which transmission/socialisation/reinforcement occurs. It is therefore important to outline or describe the ways in some detail. You should illustrate these with reference to sociological studies. However, it is also important to be able to criticise these ways or the studies you have used to support them. You should spend approximately 18 minutes on your response and aim to write at least half a side to a side of A4.

The part (d) question is worth 26 marks. The marks for this question are distributed across the three skills again: 14 are for AO1 (knowledge and understanding), 4 are for AO2a (interpretation and analysis) and 8 are for AO2b (evaluation). The question will always use the command phrase 'discuss the view' and will be followed by a sociological statement relating to how identity and/or culture might be undergoing social change. Essentially this statement will contain two positions, although one of them may be implicit in the wording of the statement. The command 'discuss' requires you to outline or describe each position in turn. However, 'discuss' also has an evaluative meaning. Therefore you must be aware of a couple of criticisms of each position too. This question is essentially an essay question and you should aim for approximately two sides of A4. Spend about 26 minutes on your response to this question.

Content Guidance

This section is intended to show you the major issues and themes covered in **The Individual and Society**. However, it does not provide an exhaustive or comprehensive list of the concepts, issues and sociological studies that you could use to answer questions on this topic. Rather, it is an outline guide that should give you a good idea of the key concepts that are essential to know and some issues and sociological studies that are worth further investigation. You should be able to access further useful information from your teacher, the textbook you are using and past copies of *Sociology Review*.

The content of The Individual and Society falls into five main areas:
- **culture, socialisation and social roles**
- **the formation and meaning of gender identities**
- **the formation and meaning of class identities**
- **the formation and meaning of ethnic identities**
- **the formation and meaning of national identities**

The topic is designed to give you a good understanding of the relationship between individuals and social structures. In particular, it aims to examine influences such as gender, social class, ethnicity, religion and the nation-state on people's sense of identity and their social behaviour — in short, how and to what extent social forces shape people. You will be expected to know the key concepts that form the foundation of these processes, especially culture, subculture, values, norms, roles, primary and secondary socialisation, and the role of their agents. With regard to gender identity, you will be expected to know about the process of gender role socialisation and how it impacts on both masculinity and femininity. With regard to social class, you need to show knowledge and understanding of a range of identities across the social class spectrum and how agencies of socialisation, particularly the family, education, the workplace and the peer group, contribute to the formation of these identities. With regard to ethnicity, you will be expected to describe the cultural characteristics of specific ethnic minority groups and to outline the role of agencies of socialisation, particularly the family, religion and the peer group, in transmitting these cultural characteristics to the next generation. Finally, you will be expected to know how institutions such as education and the media shape and reinforce national identity.

Culture, socialisation and social roles

A key aspect of The Individual and Society unit is 'conceptual confidence'. This means that it is important to become familiar with, and be able to apply accurately, key concepts that underpin the central topic areas in this unit, and to support them, whenever possible, with empirical sociological studies. You do not need detailed knowledge of sociological theory to do well in this unit, although 'theoretical awareness' of how different theories interpret aspects of the relationship between the individual and society is always useful.

Culture

- A society is a social group that normally occupies a given geographical territory and shares a sense of belonging to a common culture and set of institutions.
- Culture refers to the way of life of a social group or society. Individuals who share beliefs, values, norms, rituals, language, history and knowledge generally conform to a similar cultural outlook.
- Societies are often made up of subcultures, i.e. social groups which generally share the values and norms of mainstream society, but which may subscribe to some cultural behaviour defined as different or deviant by the majority culture (e.g. ethnic minority cultures, youth cultures).

Values and norms

- Values are beliefs and goals relating to what members of a society or culture feel is morally important and desirable, and they act as general guidelines for behaviour.
- The principal values of UK culture include respect for human life, free speech, achievement, equality of opportunity, materialism, individualism and privacy.
- Norms are the cultural expectations that societies attach to particular types of behaviour on the basis of sharing key values.

Roles and status

- Social roles are sets of norms that are culturally expected of individuals. For example, the role of mother in the contemporary UK involves expectations about how 'good' mothers should behave, and is consequently used to judge socially individuals who do not live up to these expectations.

- Status refers to the prestige attached to a particular role because members of society value highly the behaviour associated with the role. For example, doctors are held in high regard because their behaviour is directly concerned with saving lives.
- In some societies, both roles and status may be ascribed meanings that are fixed at birth by descent or inheritance, or by physical characteristics such as skin colour or gender. Norms relating to the work people do, relationships, marriage, political and economic power etc. are restricted and often unchangeable.
- In western societies, both roles and status tend to be achieved because members of society value equality of opportunity and meritocracy.
- A meritocratic society is one which rewards people on merit alone and is open to all. All social groups are protected and regulated equally in the eyes of the law.

Evaluation

- Values, norms, roles and statuses are relative to particular historical periods, societies and subcultures.
- The notion of meritocracy may be exaggerated — there is evidence that some subcultures found in the UK, particularly the working class and some ethnic minority groups, are regarded as 'inferior' and consequently they find it difficult to achieve the roles and status achieved by other groups.

Key concepts

culture; subcultures; values; norms; role; ascribed status; achieved status; meritocracy

Socialisation

- Socialisation is the learning of cultural attitudes and behaviour.
- Studies of feral children demonstrate the importance of the socialisation process, because children who lack sustained contact with other humans lack basic social skills.
- Socialisation also involves social control, i.e. once social rules have been learnt, they need to be frequently enforced through the use of positive and negative sanctions.

There are two broad types of socialisation: primary and secondary socialisation.

Primary socialisation

- Parents and families play the crucial role in primary socialisation.
- Parents transmit the values and norms necessary for children to demonstrate social competence.

- This process will result in the development of a conscience and guilt as a child learns the boundaries of acceptable and unacceptable behaviour.
- Parents act as role models and children internalise key values through imitation.
- Children's sense of identity is shaped by the social reaction of their parents.
- Children's personalities are partly shaped by culture, because most parents will follow dominant cultural norms with regard to child rearing.

Key concepts

primary socialisation; secondary socialisation; social control; positive and negative sanctions; conscience; role models; social reaction

Secondary socialisation

Whereas the principal agents of primary socialisation are parents and families, there are several agents of secondary socialisation.

The education system
- Socialisation in schools involves transmission of knowledge and skills, while key values such as achievement, individualism and competition are transmitted through streaming, sport, assemblies, speech days etc.
- Socialisation in schools, through the teaching of national identity in literature, language and history, may result in a pride in belonging to a wider social group, such as society or a religious organisation.
- Consensus sociologists (see p. 17) believe that socialisation in schools produces model pupils and citizens.
- Conflict sociologists (see p. 18) argue that schools operate a hidden curriculum that socialises subordinate social groups into ruling-class culture and the acceptance of inequality and failure as natural states.
- The national curriculum is seen by some as an attempt to socialise children into passive uncritical thinking, because it excludes critical subjects like sociology.

Evaluation

- Evidence from studies such as those carried out by Willis, Fuller etc. indicate that pupils can successfully resist the hidden curriculum.
- Not all pupils are transformed into model pupils, but nor are they turned into cultural dopes, as can be seen by the existence of anti-school subcultures and truancy.
- Moreover, outside school, there exists evidence of oppositional values in the shape of strikes, new social movements etc.

Key concepts

hidden curriculum; national curriculum; ruling-class culture; national identity

The peer group
- Peer groups are made up of people of similar social status, i.e. friends, workmates.
- The values and behaviour of such a group can influence the behaviour of individuals, especially in adolescence.

- Anti-school, delinquent and deviant subcultures may encourage young people to adopt values and norms in opposition to those of mainstream culture.
- Occupational peer groups may shape individual behaviour by imposing ethical constraints, influencing attitudes towards employers, supplying people with a strong or weak sense of class identity, stressing that community comes before the individual etc.

Evaluation

- Surveys indicate that on most issues, young people are generally in broad agreement with their parents.
- Most youth rebellion is temporary or short term.

Key concepts

peer group; anti-school culture

Religion

- Religion is a key agent of socialisation because it socialises people into moral values. These provide the guidelines that underpin other agencies of socialisation, especially the family and education.
- The transmission of religious values, especially in ethnic minority cultures, may function to integrate people into a moral community and identity.

Evaluation

- The influence of religion as an agent of socialisation may be undermined by the general national decline in religious practice and belief.
- Conflict sociologists argue that religious values are aimed primarily at persuading subordinate groups to accept the inevitability of inequalities such as poverty.

Key concepts

moral community

Mass media

- The mass media may have replaced religion in importance as a secondary agent of socialisation.
- Some media sociologists have expressed concern about the influence of media content, especially of violence, on the socialisation of young children.
- Other sociologists are concerned about the socialisation function of the media in reinforcing stereotypes — and therefore prejudice and discrimination — as regards less powerful social groups, such as women, ethnic minorities, the disabled and homosexuals.
- Conflict sociologists claim that the mass media socialise subordinate social groups into the ideology of more powerful groups.
- Postmodern sociologists claim that the mass media have socialised people into abandoning traditional sources of identity such as class and gender.
- The media in modern society socialise people into seeing their identity as shaped by style and conspicuous consumption (designer labels, fashion, logos, being seen in the right places etc.).

Evaluation

- There is no compelling evidence that media content has a negative effect upon its audience's behaviour.
- Reception analysis research indicates that young children interpret media content in a literal fashion.
- It is almost impossible to prove that media socialisation shapes people's attitudes and prejudices.
- There is little evidence that subordinate groups are taken in by ruling-class ideology.
- The view that the media socialise society's members into seeing consumption as more important than class or gender as a source of personal identity is exaggerated.

Key concepts

conspicuous consumption

The consensus approach to socialisation

A debate is going on between sociologists about the function of socialisation. Those sociologists who take a consensus view argue that all members of society agree on fundamental or core values. The function of socialisation is to make sure that all members of society are fully integrated into these common values and so share a sense of belonging. The nuclear family is the vital agency of socialisation because it transmits culture from one generation to another, so ensuring the reproduction of society and social order. The family acts as a personality factory, producing children whose behaviour is shaped by key values such as individualism and achievement. Parents benefit because they gain stability and satisfaction from the parenting experience. However, some consensus sociologists argue that socialisation in modern society is becoming less effective because of trends such as increasing divorce and the lack of a father in many one-parent families.

Evaluation

- The consensus view overestimates the success of the socialisation process, as indicated by the existence of problems such as child abuse, youth suicide and eating disorders.
- So-called common values may be the values of dominant social groups.
- This view presents an 'over-socialised' view of children. For example, children may negotiate socialisation with parents, and parents themselves may be socialised into particular ways of thinking or behaving by their children.
- It presents socialisation as a universal, homogeneous experience and consequently neglects differences due to wealth, social class, ethnicity, religion etc.
- There is no universal agreement on how socialisation should occur, as indicated by the debate about smacking children.
- There is evidence from Phoenix, Cashmore etc. that one-parent families can successfully socialise children and the absence of a father does not necessarily damage children.

consensus; core or common values

The conflict approach to socialisation

Those sociologists who take a conflict approach argue that society is composed of a variety of competing value systems, although some groups have more power than others to impose their values on subordinate groups. Value consensus therefore does not exist — it is the product of ideology, i.e. a set of ideas that aim to justify inequality. The function of socialisation is to make sure that children grow up accepting inequality, hierarchy, exploitation and patriarchy (i.e. male dominance) as natural facts of life. Socialisation is therefore about learning to conform and accepting one's lot.

- There is little agreement among conflict sociologists about the source of this inequality; some argue it is social class, others suggest it is status such as race and age, while others argue it is gender.
- This is also an over-socialised picture of human beings in that it presents socialisation as a one-way process that cannot be resisted or negotiated.
- It presents people as brainwashed cultural dopes with no freedom of choice.

conflict; power; value consensus; ideology; inequality; exploitation; hierarchy; patriarchy

The formation and meaning of gender identities

- Sex refers to biological differences between males and females, while gender refers to the cultural expectations attached to feminine and masculine roles.
- Some consensus sociologists believe that gender roles are biologically determined and therefore are fixed and unchangeable, while feminists argue that gender roles are socially constructed in traditional and patriarchal ways via gender role socialisation.
- Traditional views of masculinity emphasise that males should be physically active, authoritative, aspirational and in control of their emotions, and that they are more suited to leadership and the breadwinner role than females.
- Traditional views of femininity emphasise that females are passive, emotional, more concerned with their appearance, more adept at caring and more suited to domestic work than men. Feminists suggest that these ideas about what constitutes the 'feminine' (i.e. the mother-housewife and sex object) are defined and shaped by men.

Gender role socialisation

The family

Evidence suggests that gender identity stems from:

- imitation of parental role models
- parents rewarding gender-appropriate behaviour, i.e. manipulation
- parents discouraging gender-inappropriate behaviour, e.g. crying in boys
- parents adopting different modes of speech depending on the gender of the child
- mothers' preoccupation with female children's appearance
- parents giving children gender-specific toys, books and games, i.e. canalisation
- children being dressed in gender-appropriate clothes and colours
- parents assigning gender-specific household chores to children
- parents socially controlling the behaviour of girls more tightly than boys

Education

- Until the 1990s, the hidden curriculum transmitted gender-stereotyped assumptions about feminine behaviour through teacher expectations, timetabling of subject choices, career advice, textbook content etc. Despite increasing educational success for females in the last ten years, the persistence of gender differences in subject choices, especially in further and higher education, indicates that this may still be a problem today.
- In particular, working-class girls are still following traditional gender routes — leaving school at 16, temporary jobs, marriage, motherhood etc.
- There is some evidence that the hidden curriculum through teacher expectations may be resulting in working-class boys following traditional gender routes into manual jobs. Controlling masculine behaviour may become more important than ensuring boys receive a good education.
- Recent studies suggest that young males may reject academic work because their experience of their mothers helping them with homework and the likelihood that their primary school teacher was female means that they equate learning with femininity.

The peer group

- There is evidence that working-class boys may reject the goals of schooling and set up anti-school subcultures organised around deviant activities and the exaggeration of aspects of masculinity, e.g. aggression, toughness and risk taking.
- Mac An Ghaill suggests that such subcultures may be a reaction to a 'crisis in masculinity', as working-class boys learn that traditional working-class jobs and roles such as breadwinner and head of household are in decline.
- Membership of deviant subcultures may confer status on boys for exaggerating masculine values and norms while negatively sanctioning behaviour defined as feminine.

The mass media

Feminists are critical of a range of mass media that socialise females into either domestic or sexualised patterns of femininity:

- Popular literature, especially fairy tales and children's stories, portray females as the weaker sex and males as heroic guardians of female virtue.
- The content of children's books confirms traditional gender roles in terms of the role models offered in them.
- Comics and magazines for teenage adolescents encourage them to concentrate on appearance and romance rather than on education and careers.
- Women's magazines are apprentice manuals for motherhood and domesticity.
- Television, cinema and advertising continue to show women disproportionately in domestic roles or as appendages of successful men, and emphasise their physical looks and sex appeal at the expense of their ability or personality.
- 'New lads' and pornography assert a very traditional view of masculinity organised around interpreting women as sexual objects, sport and drinking culture.

Evaluation

- The concept of gender role socialisation is over-deterministic and paints a very over-socialised picture of children.
- Some males and females may be happy to choose traditional gender roles; as Hakim points out, some women want and enjoy the role of mother and housewife.
- Other studies point out that processes such as the hidden curriculum and the interpretation of media images are not uncritically internalised by children; they are negotiated and perhaps even resisted.
- It is difficult to prove that media images have an effect upon gender stereotyping; the family may be a more important agency of socialisation.
- The educational success of females and the feminisation of the workforce suggest that traditional gender role socialisation may not be as powerful as feminists think it is.
- The main victims of gender role socialisation according to the sociological literature seem to be working-class boys and girls; does this indicate that class is more important than gender?

Key concepts

gender role socialisation; femininity; masculinity; manipulation; canalisation; crisis in masculinity; deviant subcultures; sexual objects

New forms of femininity and masculinity

Sociologists suggest that traditional or hegemonic definitions of masculinity and femininity are in decline. New forms of femininity and masculinity are supposedly emerging, as indicated by the following:

- Surveys by Sue Sharpe and Helen Wilkinson (*Genderquake*) suggest that teenage girls' attitudes are more aspirational today compared with Sharpe's study of teenage girls in 1974, which found they stressed marriage and motherhood as their main ambitions.

- The workforce has become increasingly feminised, thus increasing women's financial and cultural power. For example, women are increasingly the main economic breadwinners in areas characterised by high male unemployment.
- Increasing cultural power may be reflected in the increase in women petitioning for divorce (they outnumber men), single-person households and voluntary childlessness.
- Surveys indicate that women are demanding more power in marriage, expect more out of their husbands and partners, and are no longer willing to put up with abuse or empty-shell marriages.
- There is some anecdotal evidence for young females adopting masculine values and norms, especially in regard to sex, drinking culture and girl gangs.
- There is increased tolerance and acceptance of homosexuality.
- An increasing number of men are choosing to be househusbands. It is argued that the emergence of a 'new man' who shares childcare and housework may be a reaction to the crisis in masculinity. This refers to the lack of traditional jobs and roles for men. They may therefore be forced to change their behaviour.
- The increasing feminisation of masculinity may be reflected in the marketing of men's cosmetics and toiletries, and the commodification of men's bodies in the media.
- Postmodernists suggest that both men and women now see consumption and leisure as the key factors in defining and shaping their identity, rather than masculinity and femininity.

Evaluation

- Change may be illusory or at best exaggerated because the evidence suggests that patriarchy is still influential, as reflected in the lack of women in top jobs and the 18% pay gap between men and women.
- Many women who work still have the dual burden of being mainly responsible for housework and childcare.
- There is a tendency in accounts of gender role socialisation to treat men's and women's experiences homogeneously and to ignore class and ethnic differences in experience. It is unlikely, for example, that working-class women experience these changes to the same degree as middle-class women.
- Men dominate consumption of leisure because they have more economic power than women and more free time.
- Men may be reacting to the crisis in masculinity in traditional ways, i.e. by turning in frustration to violence, sexism, crime, anti-subcultures based on exaggerating masculine values etc.

Key concepts

feminisation of the workforce; hegemonic masculinity; voluntary childlessness; the new man; the feminisation of masculinity; the commodification of men's bodies; consumption

The formation and meaning of class identities

Our social identity (public persona) and our sense of self (subjective awareness) are strongly bound up with our employment and workplace, and the income, status and lifestyle that arise out of it. Occupation links identity to social class because in the UK social class is categorised by official agencies such as the government on the basis of employment situation and market situation.

- Employment situation refers to the amount of power that people have over their work, i.e. whether people are employers, self-employed, employed, temporary or casual workers, whether they exercise authority over others etc.
- Market situation refers to the skills that workers have to sell in the labour market relative to other workers. Some skills attract more income, job security, promotion opportunities, status etc.
- There is evidence that class identity based upon occupation is a powerful influence on the social relationships we forge. For example, workplace peer groups are often the basis of social networks outside work.

The upper class

- A key value of this group is that economic power (wealth) is a source of opportunity, privilege and power over others, which is worth reproducing and protecting.
- Upper-class families share common social backgrounds because of inter-marriage and extended kinship networks, which are closed to outsiders.
- Children from such backgrounds are socialised into a culture of privilege organised around common attitudes, language, schools, exclusive social pursuits etc.
- Public schools socialise upper-class children into the values of conservatism, respect for tradition, nationalism and acceptance of authority and hierarchy as natural outcomes of superior breeding and upbringing.
- Public school pupils are encouraged to see themselves as an elite.
- The peer group is central because it functions outside schools as an old-boy network, which confers economic and cultural advantages on its members.

The middle classes

- Sociologists largely agree that non-manual work is characterised by distinct social class fractions, which differ in terms of economic rewards, lifestyle and cultural attitudes. These fractions are the middle classes.

content guidance

- However, according to Light, these groups do share some common suburban values including: the need to communicate social position through conspicuous consumption; home ownership; use of language; resistance to social change; respectability and decency; a sense of social difference.
- The middle-class family is child-centred and transmits achievement motivation and functional autonomy to their children.
- Bourdieu notes that experience of middle-class habitus results in the acquisition of cultural capital, which advantages the middle-class child in an educational system run by the middle classes.
- Savage notes differences between professional and managerial cultural attitudes and pursuits.
- Saunders notes differences in the cultural values of privately employed professionals compared with those employed by the state.
- Marxists like Braverman argue that white-collar workers are experiencing radical changes in the workplace due to technology, restructuring and the introduction of working practices such as those found in call centres. This has resulted in the deskilling of such workers.
- Braverman argues that deskilling has led to a reduction in pay and skill levels, and status. White-collar workers have become similar to the working class in terms of their cultural attitudes (proletarianisation).
- There are some signs that the self-employed may be adopting a more militant cultural outlook.

Evaluation

- A lack of empirical research may mean that generalisations are being made about middle-class culture.
- Marshall's survey of class attitudes found that 50% of his white-collar sample saw themselves as working class, but their attitudes and lifestyle differed from those of manual workers.

Key concepts

employment situation; market situation; culture of privilege; old-boy network; class fractions; suburban identity; achievement motivation; functional autonomy; habitus; cultural capital; deskilling; proletarianisation

The working class

- Until the late twentieth century, many working-class people subscribed to a 'proletarian traditionalist' identity that had the following characteristics:
  - They lived in tight-knit, work-based communities, an example being mining areas.
  - They had a strong awareness of their class position.
  - They saw society in terms of 'them' versus 'us'.
  - The extended family was the key agent of socialisation.

- The extended family acted as a mutual support system.
  - They had a strong sense of loyalty to the occupational peer group.
  - Community was reflected in trade union membership and working men's clubs.
- It is argued that the decline in manual work has weakened this proletarian traditionalist identity.
- Some sociologists have identified a 'deferential working class' composed of rural manual workers, whose value system stresses traditional attitudes and beliefs — respect for superior breeding, conservatism etc.
- A new working class (instrumental collectivist) has appeared. These people do not see their class as important, they define themselves through their families and they work for instrumental reasons (i.e. money/standard of living).
- High unemployment in the 1980s and 1990s has allegedly led to the emergence of an underclass characterised by an anti-work, welfare-dependent and crime-prone culture.
- Some commentators believe that working-class identity is in terminal decline, because people now judge each other on the basis of consumption of style and labels rather than on the basis of social class.

Evaluation

- A lack of recent empirical research may mean that generalisations are being made about working-class culture.
- Studies of the poor and long-term unemployed suggest that they subscribe to the same ideas about work, family and crime as everyone else.
- Marshall's survey indicates that manual workers still see social class as very important.

Key concepts

proletarian traditionalist; deferential worker; instrumental collectivist; mutual support system; extended kin; underclass; welfare dependency

The formation and meaning of ethnic identities

In the UK, the term 'ethnic minority' generally refers to people who originated in the former British colonies of the Indian subcontinent and the Caribbean.

Evaluation

- The term 'ethnic minority' implies 'alien' or 'immigrant', yet the majority of people of ethnic minority extraction living in the UK are British-born and hold British nationality.
- The use of the term 'ethnic minority' neglects the fact that many ethnic minorities are white.

- The use of the term 'ethnic minorities' ignores the fact that members of these groups have very different geographical roots, histories, religions, traditions and lifestyles.
- The term 'ethnic minority', along with 'white' and 'black', disguises differences based on social class and gender.

The meaning of ethnic identity

A number of shared cultural characteristics make up ethnic minority culture:
- common descent
- geographical roots
- shared language
- shared history
- religion
- traditions and rituals

Agents of ethnic minority socialisation

The family

- For Indian, Pakistani and Bangladeshi children, the family immerses children into the key cultural characteristics of the ethnic minority group, i.e. its religion, language and traditions, before they experience the white majority culture.
- Adolescent attitudes towards love and marriage may be qualitatively different among Muslims, Hindus and Sikhs from those experienced by white teenagers.
- The family is the central source of identity for Indian, Pakistani and Bangladeshi people. There is a strong sense of obligation to the elderly and extended kin.
- Hill found that family commitments lay at the heart of Asian communities in Leicester.
- Song found that Chinese children who wanted education rather than a career in the family takeaway were regarded as 'less Chinese' by their parents.
- Brittain suggested that African-Caribbean parents were less efficient at socialisation than their white peers, but evidence collected by Phoenix and Cashmore separately does not support this view.

Education

Studies of ethnic minority experience of education have focused on the hidden curriculum.
- Studies of hidden curriculum content suggest that ethnic minority culture and religion are rendered invisible or less important than white culture.

- Studies of teacher expectations indicate that teachers may label African-Caribbean culture as a problem because its values are seen to be in conflict with school culture.
- Studies by Troyna, Mac An Ghaill and Fuller indicate that some pupils may exaggerate aspects of African-Caribbean culture to resist racial stereotyping in schools, usually via anti-school subcultures.
- Studies of Indian children indicate the importance of educational success to family identity.

Religion

For some ethnic minority groups, particularly Indian, Pakistani, Bangladeshi and Jewish, religion is probably the most influential agent of socialisation outside the family.

- Jacobson notes that young Pakistanis see being Muslim as more important than being Pakistani or British.
- Islam has a strong impact on young Pakistani and Bangladeshi identity in terms of their diet, worship, dress, behaviour and everyday routines and practices.
- Gardner and Shukur see Islam as compensating for the racism experienced by ethnic minority groups on an everyday basis.
- Young African-Caribbean involvement in the Rastafarian movement may be a defensive strategy to help cope with white racism.

The peer group

- African-Caribbeans may use gangsta rap and hip-hop as a means of coping with the racism and deprivation of everyday urban existence.
- African-Caribbeans may assert black pride and history through urban protest such as riots.
- Tony Sewell suggests that young African-Caribbeans are overly influenced by commercial popular culture and its emphasis on designer labels and logos in constructing a personal identity.

White culture

The reaction of the white majority culture to ethnic minority culture is an important influence on socialisation:

- Surveys suggest that one-third of the British population admit to being racially prejudiced.
- Modood found that ethnic minority members saw themselves as British, but were not comfortable with such an identity because they felt that a majority of white people did not accept them as British.

Ethnic minority culture: potential change

A lack of empirical evidence characterises this area, but the following sociological observations can be made:

- There are increasing tensions in some parts of the UK as young Asians, especially Muslim youth, assert their religious identity, usually in defensive reaction to racist actions.
- There are increasing tensions between different ethnic minority groups, e.g. Hindus and Muslims, who rarely mix socially.
- There may be generational conflict between ethnic minority parents and children as the latter come into contact with their white peers and want to adopt western values with regard to education, marriage etc.
- Butler found that young Islamic women subscribed to quite different identities from their mothers in respect of equality, domestic roles, fashion and marriage.
- Song noted generational tensions in Chinese families as children seek education rather than employment in the family restaurant.
- Mixed marriages and relationships between African-Caribbeans and whites continue to increase, e.g. 50% of black men have white partners.
- Johal notes the 'dual identity' of many young Asians, who inherit an Asian identity but adopt elements of white culture, especially in the company of their white peers.

Evaluation

- Ethnic identity will be influenced by social class and race.
- Butler found that young female Muslims were generally happy with the way Islam treated women.
- Generational conflict over arranged marriages is probably exaggerated by the white media.

Key concepts

ethnic minority; racism; prejudice; discrimination; institutional racism; generational conflict; dual identity; hybrid cultures

The formation and meaning of national identities

- National identity is the feeling of being part of a larger community, the nation, which gives people a sense of purpose, meaning and belonging.
- National identity often intersects with ethnic identity.

- Sociologists believe that national identity is a social construction and is made up of the following characteristics:
  - a shared sense of history and traditions
  - ritual and ceremonies that commemorate sharing and belonging
  - customs relating to dress and food
  - fervent support at sporting occasions such as the Olympics or World Cup
  - assumptions about national character, e.g. the British are supposedly noted for decency and fair play
  - the construction of national heroes and myths
  - symbols, e.g. the Union Jack
- British identity, in addition to the above, is the result of:
  - geography — the UK's island status clearly distinguishes it from Europe
  - religion — the UK is predominantly Protestant
  - history — the British empire united the elites of England, Wales and Scotland in a common imperial goal
  - the monarchy
  - the existence of democratic rights such as free speech
  - parliamentary democracy

Key socialising agents

- Education systems celebrate aspects of national identity through choice of curriculum content — English literature and language, history etc.
- The mass media, especially the tabloids, positively focus on the role of the monarchy and encourage excessive patriotism during war and sporting events like the World Cup.
- Television reporting of national events and rituals such as state occasions and royal marriages/funerals contributes to pride in national identity.

British identity and social change

British identity may be fragmenting for a number of reasons:
- Devolution of power in Northern Ireland, Wales and Scotland has seen Celtic identity reasserting itself.
- European influence is growing through such mechanisms as the introduction of the euro.
- The multicultural nature of the UK and racist reactions to ethnic minority presence may result in ethnic and religious identities being adopted at the expense of British identity.

- Globalisation blurs the meaning of national identity as popular culture, diet, fashion, music etc. are influenced by our easy access to a diversity of international influences.

Evaluation

- There is little empirical research relating to how people feel about their national identity.
- The intensity of national identity may be tempered by social class, ethnicity and gender, e.g. men may have stronger feelings of patriotism than women because they are culturally expected to express it through traditionally masculine mechanisms such as sport.
- Some of the concepts used in this debate are notoriously difficult to define and measure, e.g. globalisation.

Key concepts

nation; patriotism; Celtic identity; globalisation; multiculturalism; devolution; diversity

Questions
&
Answers

This section of the guide provides you with six questions on the topic of **The Individual and Society** in the style of the OCR examination. The first three questions are followed by a grade-C candidate response. These are on the right track but fail, for various reasons, to score very high marks. Questions 1–5 have a grade-A response. It is important to note that these are not 'model' answers. These responses are not the only possible answers to these questions, nor are they necessarily the best. They represent one particular successful style; one that answers the question set and demonstrates the appropriate skills, especially using suitable concepts and studies, displaying a critical and evaluative awareness towards the material used, and presenting a logically structured argument.

You must therefore not make the mistake of learning the A-grade responses parrot-fashion. Remember that you have to be flexible and to be able to respond to the specific demands of a question. It would be quite possible, particularly in the answers to (c) and (d), to take a different approach, or to use different material, or even to come to a different conclusion, and still gain very high marks.

A sixth question is provided which is not accompanied by a student answer. It is followed by a plan of action, and you should use this to write your own response. It is recommended that you spend some time revising the topic before tackling this question. You should answer the question under timed conditions with no notes.

Examiner's comments

The candidate answers are accompanied by examiner's comments. These are preceded by the icon *e* and indicate where credit is due. For the grade-A answers, the examiner shows you what it is that enables the candidate to score so highly. Particular attention is given to the candidate's use of the examinable skills: knowledge and understanding; interpretation and analysis; and evaluation. For the grade-C answers, the examiner points out areas for improvement, specific problems and common errors. You are also invited to rewrite the answer in order to gain higher marks, and some pointers are given to show you how you might do this.

The formation and meaning of class identities (I)

Item A

The upper-class family is an important agency of socialisation because it immerses its children in a culture of privilege which clearly distinguishes this class from other social groups. Upper-class norms include the employment of nannies and other domestic staff, participation in blood sports such as fox-hunting and concern with etiquette (i.e. rules about social behaviour, dress etc.). The culture of private schooling and the social networking of peer groups that continue into adult life, i.e. 'the old-boy network', reinforce this socialisation process.

(a) **Identify and briefly explain two characteristics of upper-class culture mentioned in Item A.** (8 marks)

(b) **Identify and briefly explain two ways in which ascribed status differs from achieved status.** (8 marks)

(c) **Outline and briefly evaluate two ways in which experience of education may reinforce class identity.** (18 marks)

(d) **Discuss the view that social class is the main influence on people's identity in the contemporary UK.** (26 marks)

Total: 60 marks

■ ■ ■

Answer to question 1: grade-C candidate

(a) The upper classes enjoy taking part in blood sports. This means they are into fox-hunting and shooting birds. The working classes do not take part in these types of sports. They prefer spectator sports such as football.

> *e* The candidate identifies an appropriate cultural characteristic from the data but fails to make the most of the explanation. There is an attempt to contrast leisure activities across social classes, but the explanation needed to focus on why the upper classes indulge in particular types of sport.

The second characteristic of the upper classes is their accents. They tend to have posher accents than the rest of us. For example, they are said to speak the Queen's English. They don't have regional accents.

> *e* Unfortunately accent is not included in Item A. The instruction in the question quite clearly says 'mentioned in Item A', so the candidate cannot be rewarded for this point. The candidate scores 2 out of 8 marks.

question

(b) One difference between an ascribed status and an achieved status is that ascribed status is pre-determined before birth. Therefore when you are born you would take on the status of your mother if you were a girl and your father if you were a boy. Achieved status, however, is based on your own merit — you work for your status.

e This response successfully identifies a difference and attempts to develop an explanation. This is partially successful. The answer would have picked up full marks if it had developed some examples of what roles were expected of male and female ascribed status.

Another difference between the two is that achieved status is associated with social class whereas ascribed status is to do with inherited wealth or poverty.

e The candidate just about scrapes a difference but fails to follow up with an explanation and illustration. The candidate scores 4 out of 8 marks.

(c) The upper classes go to public schools. These are private schools which confirm to children from these backgrounds that they are wealthy, special and superior to other social classes. For example, they learn leadership skills in these schools and socialise with other rich kids, which may make them think that their culture is somehow dominant. They also learn how to understand opera, classical music and ballet so that their culture is seen as more intelligent than the popular culture enjoyed by the masses. However, their culture is no better than anyone else's — it's just that they've got the power to tell us what is good and what is bad.

e This is an interesting paragraph that successfully identifies public schools as a 'way'. The outline needed more detail and a reference to a sociological study, but it does make some pertinent points about superiority, leadership skills and, implicitly, high culture. The evaluation, however, is weak. It is more of a value judgement than a critique of the way in which experience of education reinforces class identity.

Working-class children may have their working-class identity reinforced by teacher labelling. Some teachers stereotype children. They believe that certain types of children, e.g. working-class and black children, are not very bright. In the class-room, they might show that they think this by treating working-class children in a poor way. Such working-class children may end up in bottom streams, feeling very resentful of their treatment. They might turn to anti-school activities by acting up in working-class ways. However, although there are lots of working-class kids in the bottom streams, this might have more to do with poverty or poor parents than being at school. These pupils may not be aware that they are working class or that teachers don't like them because they are working class.

e A relevant way is recognised and there is a reasonable attempt at outlining the role of education in reinforcing working-class identity. However, the answer is very assertive in places, despite its grounding in labelling theory. It does not acknowledge any evidence in the form of studies. There is an attempt at evaluation, but it is assertive and speculative rather than sociological. In general, however, it is not a bad response. It scores 6 out of 10 marks for knowledge and under-standing and 3 out of 4 for interpretation and analysis because it consistently addresses the question and is therefore focused. It scores 2 out of 4 for its evaluation, which tends to be speculative rather than sociological in nature. The answer to part (c) scores 11 out of 18 marks.

(d) It is said today that social class is no longer the most important source of an individual's identity. Some think that the boundaries of class are being eroded and that society is becoming classless. It is said that the media and our consumer culture now provide us with all the identity we need and therefore traditional influences like social class, community and family are less impor-tant in people's lives.

e This is not a bad introduction. It sets the scene for the debate and identifies two competing positions.

Some sociologists argue that certain jobs are likely to result in a greater sense of class identity than others. Manual work and particularly mining is often dangerous and workers think of themselves as a community which should stick together through thick and thin. As a result, miners are very proud to be working class.

e The candidate fails to mention any studies in this section. This is a shame, as the points raised are valid but they are undermined by their common-sense character.

Middle-class people are less likely to have developed a class identity according to Savage. Nevertheless, they do have a common culture with distinct values and norms, e.g. keeping up with the Joneses, an obsession with respectability and decency etc. Savage argues that middle-class professionals pass on these values to their children. He calls this cultural capital.

e This paragraph is a distinct improvement on the last. The point about middle-class identity is accurately referenced. The candidate uses the concept of common culture well but is less successful in using the concept of cultural capital.

Some sociologists have focused on how being working class may affect working-class youth identity. Williams found that working-class youth found football hooli-ganism attractive because it allowed them the opportunity of exaggerating working-class values by being seen to be tough, strong and hard. Jefferson found a similar attitude among skinheads in the 1970s. They dressed in a working-class way with Doc Martens, braces etc. in order to celebrate their working-class roots. Willis too showed how working-class boys rejected school values in favour of their own class values.

e Here is an excellent paragraph that makes very valid points about how youth might interpret working-class identity. The studies are used in an excellent fashion. This is a good example of applied sociology.

However, it is important to note that class may no longer be the main influence on people's identity in the UK today. Ethnic minorities may see their culture or

religion as more important. Jacobson found that Pakistani youth in his study said that Islam was more important than being working class.

e This section is both focused on the question and evaluative. It makes an excellent point about culture and religions as alternative sources of identity, and illustrates it with an excellent example of an empirical study.

Finally, some sociologists say class is dead or that it is no longer important. It is said that in modern societies we get our identity from the media and popular culture.

e This paragraph has the potential for evaluation, but fails to develop either of the two points made. In particular, the reference to media and popular culture is too vague.

e This is a reasonably good response to part (d). It displays a sound knowledge and understanding of the debate, although it is a little unbalanced. It perhaps needed to develop in more detail the points about culture, religion and particularly media and popular culture. However, it deals with concepts well throughout and confidently uses empirical studies to support its case. It therefore scores 11 out of 14 marks for knowledge and understanding. In terms of interpretation and analysis, the candidate focuses on the debate and applies a range of ideas, concepts and studies to it: the answer consequently scores 3 marks out of 4 for these skills. Alternatives to class are offered but there needs to be more explicit evaluation of these, especially the role of popular culture and media. The candidate scores 3 out of 8 marks for evaluation, making a total of 17 out of 26 for part (d).

Overall mark: 34/60

Task

Examine part (d) carefully and think about how you might improve it with brief references to:

(a) gender
(b) youth
(c) consumption

■ ■ ■

Answer to question 1: grade-A candidate

(a) Firstly, Item A refers to the employment of domestic servants such as nannies and other domestic staff. The latter will probably be made up of butlers, maids, gardeners, chauffeurs etc. The existence of such staff will reinforce the hierarchical nature of upper-class culture and feelings of superiority over those who do not have access to such domestic support.

e The candidate wisely focuses on a characteristic that is clearly part of Item A. There is a good attempt to extend the range of examples of domestic staff identified. Moreover, the explanation is focused on analysing how the existence of domestic staff supports aspects of upper-class culture. This is reasonably convincing.

Secondly, the culture of private schooling, especially education at public schools such as Eton, is a common characteristic of upper-class culture. Children spend long periods of time away from home, boarding at schools which charge fees which are often the equivalent of an average manual worker's annual wage.

> *e* Again, the candidate concentrates on a characteristic that is clearly visible in the data. The explanation, however, focuses on facts about private schooling rather than briefly analysing how it might contribute to upper-class culture. The item talks about the 'culture of private schooling' — this response neglects that cultural aspect. Overall, however, this is a good response that scores **6 out of 8** marks.

(b) First of all, ascribed status is something over which people have no control. It is a type of status which is usually inherited and largely unchangeable. For example, in some ethnic minority cultures and religions, gender may be ascribed because men and women are allocated very different roles according to their sex. For example, only men can be the head of household or religious leaders. Achieved status, on the other hand, is regarded as the product of individual achievement. It is the result of education and hard work and, in principle, is potentially possible for everyone regardless of gender, social class etc.

> *e* The candidate clearly displays knowledge and understanding of both ascribed and achieved status, and illustrates this in detail. Most importantly, the examiner can clearly see that the candidate has distinguished between the different types of status.

Secondly, ascribed status carries with it a rigid set of cultural values, norms and roles, which means that people's sense of identity and behaviour is very predictable. For example, in ascribed subcultures, marriage is an institution which is strictly controlled by rules which govern who people can marry and when. In achievement-orientated subcultures, no such rules in principle exist. People can marry who they want. For example, even those people with ascribed status in the UK, e.g. Prince Charles, can marry commoners. Behaviour in modern societies like the UK is therefore less predictable than that in ascribed societies, and consequently identity and behaviour in the UK is characterised by greater diversity and choice.

> *e* This is a sophisticated response. A grade-A response does not have to be so detailed, but this is a very good example of a candidate who clearly understands the material. The candidate scores **8 out of 8** marks.

(c) Evidence from studies of upper-class education in public schools suggests that schools play a major role in reinforcing class identity. There is evidence that public schools promote the values of conservatism, nationalism and acceptance of authority and hierarchy as natural outcomes of superior breeding. Public school-boys are encouraged to see themselves as the elite. Studies of these schools, e.g. Debra Roker, suggest that private school pupils see themselves as superior to the products of state schools. Roker also found that they see the poor as responsible for their own poverty.

> *e* The candidate could have chosen from a variety of examples relating to class. This

question

is a good example to use because public schools are central agencies of socialisation into upper-class culture. The candidate uses an empirical study to support this case. The use of sociological studies in answering this part of the question is highly recommended.

However, our sociological knowledge of public school culture is based on very few empirical studies. Roker's findings relate to a private girls' school and may not be typical of other private schools, especially the public schools. Much sociology in this area, therefore, may be speculative rather than hard empirical fact.

e It is perfectly legitimate to evaluate the research methods used to collect information because this challenges the validity of the 'way' identified.

Education may reinforce working-class identity too. Paul Willis found that the lads he studied were not interested in education or qualifications because they had set their minds on factory jobs. However, this did not mean that they played truant from school. The lads actually enjoyed going to school because they could have a laugh at the expense of the teachers and conformist pupils. They did this by exaggerating working-class values such as toughness, masculinity, sexism etc. Confrontation with authority actually increased respect from their peers and led to status. The school experience therefore reinforced their working-class identity and acted as a sort of rehearsal for the sorts of values and norms they expected to be expressing at work in a factory.

e The candidate makes good use of another sociological study. It is clearly related to class identity and is detailed in its illustration.

There is no doubt that schools play a role in reinforcing working-class identity but it is likely that the main influences on working-class identity are family life and occupational subcultures rather than education. Most working-class kids conform at school rather than resist it by expressing aspects of working-class culture.

e The candidate outlines another good evaluative point which stresses the importance of other agencies of socialisation and the danger of generalising to all working-class pupils. This candidate scores 10 marks for knowledge and under-standing. Both interpretation and analysis skills and evaluation skills are very well developed and the candidate scores 8 marks out of a possible 8. The candidate scores the full 18 marks for this part of the question.

(d) It can be argued that most people's identities are the product of the type of work they do and the occupational subcultures to which they belong. When we meet somebody for the first time we are likely to ask about the job they do. We may not realise it but by doing so we are probably making judgements about their status. In other words, we use occupation to categorise other people and ourselves into social classes. Evidence suggests that our class position may shape our behaviour in regard to education, health, leisure and lifestyle.

e This is a good introduction that focuses on making clear the importance of social class to people's sense of identity. It is slightly assertive and therefore needs to be supported very soon by sociological data or evidence.

If we examine the working class, we can see three distinct types of working-class identity. Parkin identifies a deferential working class largely made up of workers who have close relationships with their employers. The values of such workers are organised around the view that the world is a natural hierarchy and those at the top (i.e. their employers) are somehow born to rule. Respect for authority and a belief in ascribed status is also characteristic of the culture of this group, which is mainly found in small towns, especially rural communities.

e The candidate clearly identifies a social group whose culture is influenced by the nature of its class relationships with others. Concepts like values and ascribed status are used accurately. The points made are clearly referenced to a valid sociological study.

Secondly, studies of traditional working-class communities such as *Coal Is Our Life* by Dennis, Henriques and Slaughter suggest that manual workers like miners have a very strong sense of their class position. Working-class culture is community-based in that workers feel a very strong sense of loyalty and obligation to each other and see themselves as a distinct group in conflict with employers and managers. This sense of 'them' versus 'us' is reflected in mass membership of trade unions, voting for the political party which represents their class interests (the old Labour Party) and a mutual support system underpinned by close relationships with extended kin. Paul Willis' work on factory life identifies physical bravery and strength, masculinity and skills gained through experience rather than education as typical working-class values.

e This is an excellent section which demonstrates a range of knowledge about working-class culture and the role of social class. Two sociological studies are referenced in a convincing fashion.

Some commentators have noted that such communities are in decline because the numbers employed in traditional industries such as mining and shipbuilding have considerably fallen. Therefore it is argued that this type of class identity, which Goldthorpe called 'proletarian traditionalist', is in decline because its economic basis (i.e. manual work) has weakened.

e The candidate sees the need for an evaluative tone.

Thirdly, research has identified a 'new' form of working class. Devine's research indicated that workers of this type do not see work as the defining feature of their life. Rather they see work as a means to an end. This type of worker is instrumentalist in attitude, i.e. work is not expected to be satisfying but merely a means of providing a standard of living. Family, consumption and lifestyle shape the workers' identity. Consequently, they have no heightened sense of class awareness, loyalty or political allegiance.

question

> The candidate focuses on the central argument in the question and challenges it by referring to a third type of 'working class' in which class identity is not a priority.

In addition to research into working-class identity, research has also uncovered a range of different types of middle-class identity. Savage notes key cultural differences between professionals whose culture values knowledge, qualifications and the passing on of cultural capital to their children, and managers whose culture values standard of living and leisure pursuits. Studies of upper-class identity suggest that members of this class have a very powerful sense of identity. The concentration of wealth in the hands of the few leads to awareness among the upper class that economic power is a tremendous source of opportunity, privilege and power which is worth reproducing and protecting. Children born into this class learn that they belong to a distinct culture of privilege, which clearly marks out their social superiority and views other classes as subordinate. Such a culture is reinforced by private schooling and an old-boy network.

> The candidate takes the discussion beyond working-class identity and sees the need to examine other social class groups. Note that there is so much information to access that the candidate has made the sensible decision to spend less time on these groups. This is perfectly legitimate considering the candidate has only 30 minutes to answer this question. Therefore, most of the material in this section is an optional extra, although a good response will always make some brief reference to both the upper and middle classes.

In recent years, some sociologists have argued that these class identities are becoming less important because both the economy and society have drastically changed. In particular, the decline in manufacturing and the increase in service sector jobs such as employment in call centres have allegedly changed the nature of work so that workers no longer look to their jobs for satisfaction or identity. People are increasingly looking for identity outside occupation and class. Postmodern identity is more likely to be influenced by popular culture and the diversity and choice that characterises mass consumption. The search for style through brands and logos is said to be the main influence on young people's identity today.

> This candidate clearly understands that to 'discuss' means evaluating the argument that class is central to identity in the 'contemporary' UK. The reference to theory, although not compulsory, is accurate and there is a clear explanation of why class identity might have been replaced by identity based on consumption.

Other sociologists note that feminine identity has become more important in recent years because of increasing opportunities in the job market. Sociologists such as Mason note that ethnic minority subcultures may see their identity wrapped up in their culture and religion, especially if the majority culture discriminates against them.

> Good points are made here about the importance of gender and ethnicity as sources of identity.

Finally some sociologists argue that these ideas about consumption are exaggerated. They point out that consumption and style are superficial and temporary indicators of identity. Marshall's survey indicates that many manual workers still see social class as the most important influence in their lives. Marshall argues that class has not declined in importance. People still use it to judge others alongside gender, age and ethnic identities. He also criticises postmodernists for neglecting the fact that consumption is dependent upon having both a job and an income.

🖉 A good conclusion is offered, using empirical evidence to take the evaluation one step further, i.e. by evaluating the consumption argument.

🖉 An excellent level and range of conceptual and empirical knowledge are demonstrated in part (d), and the candidate scores 14 marks for knowledge and understanding. In addition, the candidate sustains an analysis and debate consistently and the key question is addressed throughout. The candidate therefore scores 4 marks for interpretation and analysis. Evaluation is specifically focused in a balanced way on all sides of the argument. The candidate consequently scores 8 marks for evaluation. The full 26 marks are therefore awarded for this part of the question.

Overall mark: 58/60

The formation and meaning of gender identities (I)

Item A

Comics endorse traditional feminine and masculine gender roles. The titles of boys' comics centre on action and interests like sport, war and football and feature adventure stories about men who are strong, brave and oppressive. Anything can happen to the characters involved, but it is always exciting, taking place in far-off countries, or in the past, or in a war. The boys take enormous risks and find themselves in amazing predicaments, which they come out of successfully. There are no girls, or if they do appear, their part of the story is insignificant.

(a) Using Item A only, identify and briefly explain two values associated with masculinity which are promoted by boys' comics. (8 marks)

(b) Identify and briefly explain two characteristics traditionally associated with femininity in the UK. (8 marks)

(c) Outline and briefly evaluate two ways in which the family reinforces traditional gender divisions and identities. (18 marks)

(d) Discuss the view that a variety of feminine and masculine identities have emerged in recent years in the contemporary UK. (26 marks)

Total: 60 marks

■ ■ ■

Answer to question 2: grade-C candidate

(a) Interests like sport, war and football; being brave.

> *ℓ* This answer is too brief to allow the examiner to know for sure what the student is thinking. It is not clear why the student believes the two things are values because there is no explanation, despite it being demanded by the question. In fact, 'interests like sport, war and football' is closer to a norm rather than a value and consequently gains no marks. 'Being brave' is a value associated with masculinity to some extent and gains 2 marks. The candidate scores 2 out of 8 marks.

(b) Femininity is traditionally associated by society with the home, especially the mother-housewife role. Some men believe that women's domestic skills are the product of nature and genetics. However, feminist sociologists argue instead that such roles are socially constructed, especially the family, through the primary socialisation process, e.g. through girls playing with dolls and being forced to help mum with the washing up. Boys, on the other hand, learn that their future role will be providing for their family.

> 🖉 This part of the answer very clearly identifies a traditional feminine characteristic and explains it well, using concepts such as primary socialisation, social construction and feminism. Moreover, this candidate illustrates the point by comparing it with an alternative point of view, i.e. the role of nature and masculinity (boys' future role).

Girls are also supposed to be passive compared with boys. For example, they are supposed to wait for boys to ask them out. Girls who are too aggressive might be labelled as 'pushy'.

> 🖉 The characteristic identified, i.e. 'passivity', is fine, but the example requires further development. The illustration does use a sociological concept, i.e. 'labelling', but it is unclear who is negatively defining the female behaviour. The word 'pushy' is lacking in sociological clarity and is a little commonsensical. This part of the response gains only 2 marks: 1 for identification and 1 for explanation. The candidate scores 6 out of 8 marks for part (b).

(c) The family is the primary agent of socialisation and is responsible for reinforcing traditional ideas about gender. For example, Oakley argues that parents reward gender-appropriate behaviour such as boisterousness in boys and gentility in girls. She calls this manipulation. They also discourage gender-inappropriate behaviour, e.g. crying in boys. However, despite these attempts to channel boys and girls into certain types of behaviour, there is evidence that girls are more assertive today than they were 30 years ago, which suggests that traditional gender role socialisation may be changing. For example, mothers who have careers may be strongly encouraging their daughters to compete aggressively with boys for qualifications, university places and jobs. Exam results would suggest that they are successful at this.

> 🖉 This is an excellent paragraph which uses Oakley's ideas well to illustrate how traditional gender role socialisation allegedly works. However, the evaluation clearly challenges the determinism of the Oakley argument, and although it does not quote empirical studies, the examples cited are valid.

According to Delamont, another way the family socialises children into gender roles, and which happens throughout their childhood and teenage years, is by buying them toys, games and books. Parental views on what children should play with are usually very traditional. So, for example, parents will not buy dolls for their boys unless, of course, it is Action Man. Parents also have some funny ideas about what they think girls will like. It is very rare that a girl will be bought a Lego or Meccano set because parents believe boys are more suited to such technical toys. Despite some parents' attempts to move away from traditional gendered roles by buying children neutral toys, manufacturers and toy shops are still very traditional. In addition, contact with other children and their toys makes it almost impossible for children to avoid playing with gendered toys.

 The candidate does identify a very appropriate way in which the family socialises children into gender roles and cites a valid sociological study. However, the outline is disappointing because it is very assertive in its points about toys and often does little more than state what is common sense. It requires a focused sociological grounding and would have benefited from sustained reference to Delamont and Sharpe, for example. The evaluative point is a little assertive but relevant and valid.

This candidate scores 8 marks out of 10 for knowledge and understanding because two ways in which the family reinforces traditional gender division and identities are identified and explained with reference to studies. There is a slight tendency to be overassertive and anecdotal in tone. The candidate addresses the question in a consistently focused fashion and selects a range of concepts reasonably well in order to analyse the role of the family. The candidate is awarded 3 marks out of 4 for interpretation and analysis. There is a reasonably good attempt to construct an evaluation using concepts and trends which earns 3 marks out of a possible 4 for evaluation. The candidate scores 14 marks out of 18 for this part of the question.

(d) In my view, there are a variety of different types of femininity and masculinity in Britain today.

 Part (d) requires an essay response and this candidate makes the fundamental mistake of neglecting to develop an essential part of an essay, i.e. an introduction that would set the scene. The statement in the title is a 'view' that may not be shared by others. It is very likely that such a view is part of a general sociological debate. It is often worth setting out the major players in that debate in an introduction. This candidate makes the mistake of identifying automatically with the view contained in the title. This is going to weaken the essay because it is now unlikely that the candidate will examine what gender roles were like before the 'recent' changes. In a desire to agree with the 'view', it is also likely that no sustained evaluation of the 'view' will be developed. This is one of the key aspects of the command word 'discuss'.

If we take femininity, for example, we can see that it is no longer the case that young females want to follow their mums into marriage and motherhood. Females today want more out of life. They want careers and financial independence.

 So far, this is very assertive and consequently is reading like the student's opinion or something read in a newspaper. It lacks sociological grounding in terms of data or reference to studies such as those by Sue Sharpe and Helen Wilkinson.

There is evidence for this. Chandler talks about an increase in voluntary childlessness, and the latest household statistics show that the number of single-person households has increased in recent years. Much of this increase is among young females.

 This section is a distinct improvement. The reference to Chandler is fine and there is a reference to a valid social trend.

Even among married women, we can see that traditional ideas about women being mothers and housewives, and putting up with men ordering them about, are being abandoned. More and more women are going out to work and insisting that men share the housework and the childcare. There is evidence too that women are using divorce more than men to get their independence. One reason for this is that our attitude towards femininity has changed and we no longer condemn single mothers.

e The candidate reverts to assertion again, which is a shame because seeds of sociological analysis are being shown in this paragraph. For example, the points about women going out to work and more women suing for divorce are valid, although the link to new femininities is not clear and the points are not backed up with any evidence in the form of data or studies. The final sentence in this paragraph is also very contentious.

There is also evidence that girls are becoming more like men. Celebrities like Sara Cox boast about their exploits in relation to drinking and sex in much the same way as men. Also girl gangs which are involved in violence and stealing are becoming more common in the inner cities.

e The candidate seems intent on travelling even further down the anecdotal road. There is little here that is convincing. The point about girl gangs needed to be backed up with evidence.

Some sociologists argue that in the contemporary UK, old-fashioned things like class, gender and ethnicity are no longer the main influences on our identity. They argue that people are now more concerned with consuming leisure and making sure they are seen wearing the right logos, drinking the right drinks, being seen in the right clubs etc. These sociologists believe that women are more interested in stressing these things in their life rather than stressing they are women. This new type of femininity therefore means that gender is not used to judge people any more. A good example of this is the dance scene. Thornton points out that males and females who take part in this scene treat each other as equals. It is the music and dancing that is important rather than trying to pick up the opposite sex. Gender is not an issue at these events.

e In this paragraph, the candidate becomes more sociologically focused and makes some relevant observations about postmodernism (although the term is not used). The candidate correctly identifies the view that consumption is now allegedly central to modern identity and links it in a reasonably satisfactory manner to changing femininity. The candidate uses an excellent example, i.e. the dance scene, and intelligently uses a sociological study to illustrate the general point. The inclusion of more studies to support the other points would have been useful.

Men have experienced change too. The international recession means that they can no longer guarantee that they can perform their traditional roles as breadwinners and heads of households. They may be unemployed and be unable to provide for their families. They may kill themselves because this is a slight upon their masculinity.

e This paragraph is a missed opportunity. The content indicates that the candidate is aware of modern pressures on men and masculinity, but is unable to develop this in a convincing sociological way. Instead the explanation is very generalised and no sociological study or evidence is cited in support. The student has the opportunity here to develop Mac An Ghaill's ideas about the crisis in masculinity and its implications, but instead opts for common-sense assertions about suicide.

It can be concluded that in society today gender is less important than ever before for identity. New types of femininity and masculinity have appeared which now compete with the idea that women should be mothers and men should be bread-winners. Not everyone agrees with this. Feminists still think gender is important, but very few girls call themselves feminists today.

e This is a disappointing conclusion which confirms our initial observation that this candidate has fallen 'hook, line and sinker' for the view contained in the essay title, and consequently is unwilling or unable to consider alternative views. There is an evaluative point in the final sentence, but it is limited. The candidate fails to use knowledge of feminism to challenge the view that there is variety or that women's lives have improved because of the alleged variety. Other possible influences, such as social class and ethnicity, are ignored altogether.

e The answer to part (d) displays some knowledge and understanding of femininity, masculinity and associated concepts, but it is largely descriptive. It also needed to link the points it did make more firmly to both traditional and changing forms of femininity and masculinity. A major weakness is its failure to ground the points it makes in the context of empirical studies. It therefore scores 8 marks out of a possible 14 for knowledge and understanding. The range of issues covered is quite wide, but the response is both overly assertive and focused disproportionately on femininity. The candidate consequently scores 2 marks out of 4 for interpretation and analysis. Finally, the candidate uncritically accepts the view embodied in the title and fails to develop any sustained evaluation, scoring 4 out of a possible 8 marks for this skill. The candidate scores 14 marks out of 26 for part (d).

Overall mark: 36/60

Task

Using the basic structure of this answer, rewrite it so that it would gain higher marks. The following points will help you:

- Write an opening paragraph that sets the scene for the debate, i.e. that outlines the thr ee main arguments: traditionalists, like Norman Dennis, who believe that gender is fixed and unchangeable, and who believe that changing femininities and masculinities are undermining society; feminists who believe that femininity and masculinity are socially constructed through a process of gender role socialisation;

and those sociologists who believe that a variety of femininities and masculinities have emerged in recent years.

- Now write 3–4 paragraphs, firstly outlining the characteristics associated with traditional forms of masculinity and femininity and, secondly, briefly demonstrating how agencies of socialisation function to transmit and reinforce gender roles. Take care to avoid repeating the points you have already made in answering part (c).
- Write 3–4 paragraphs outlining, with evidence, examples of new forms of femininity that have allegedly emerged in recent years. It is important to support the points you make with sociological studies and/or data. For example, you could focus on the attitudes of young women by referencing the work of Sharpe, Wilkinson, Skeggs etc. You might also focus on changes in women's attitudes towards the family, especially in regard to divorce, domestic violence, sharing childcare, voluntary childlessness, single-person households etc. Remember to link these to sociological studies and data. Thirdly, outline the view using the available evidence that consumption has undermined gender as a source of identity and created a new form of femininity in which gender is neutralised.
- Write two paragraphs examining the evidence in regard to new forms of masculinity. Mac An Ghaill and Bob Connell are very useful here. You might want to access the studies of masculinity outlined by David Abbott's 'Identity and new masculinities' in *Sociology Review*, September 2000.
- Write a conclusion evaluating the view that new forms of femininity and masculinity are emerging in the contemporary UK. Take each gender in turn and think about (a) what sociologists who believe that gender is linked to biology might say about changing femininities and masculinities; (b) what feminism might say about the notion of a 'new woman' whose lifestyle revolves around a career and conspicuous consumption; (c) how concepts like social class and ethnicity might undermine the view; and (d) how the social and economic changes affecting men may actually reinforce traditional values.

■ ■ ■

Answer to question 2: grade-A candidate

(a) Stories for boys usually stress the value of achievement in a variety of fields, e.g. abroad, in war, in space etc., which is the result of taking firm action or being assertive. Much of this action is violent and aggressive. For example, Item A suggests that males are portrayed as coming out of all sorts of exciting and dangerous situations very successfully.

Item A also implies that strength and bravery are valued in men. Supporters of traditional masculinity see this as a central feature of men as protectors, i.e. safeguarding their women and children from external threats.

e The candidate makes the most of the item in order to identify and construct a full explanation of the values inherent in boys' comics, and scores the full 8 marks.

(b) Traditionally femininity has been associated with domesticity, i.e. women have been seen as primarily responsible for the housework and especially childcare. It can be argued that parenting in the UK is most likely to be associated with mothering rather than fathering because it is assumed that women who have children should take most of the responsibility for their upbringing.

e Here we see a good, succinct example of a characteristic that clearly explains why one aspect of that characteristic exists.

Femininity is also associated with the sexual objectification of women. This refers to the fact that females are mainly judged by their attractiveness, physical figure and potential for sex, by men. As a result, a woman finds herself defined by a man in terms of her body parts rather than as a woman with a mind and personality of her own. The media confirm this and bombard society with images of women which define social standards for physical beauty and sexual attractiveness. Women are encouraged to view their bodies as a project in constant need of improvement. It is believed that such images may create the conditions in which eating disorders may flourish.

e This is an excellent response in terms of knowledge and understanding of socio-logical concepts. However, full marks can be gained with less detail. Overall, the response scores the full **8 marks**.

(c) Oakley identifies two aspects of gender role socialisation in the family which are central to reinforcing traditional divisions and identities. Firstly, she focuses on 'manipulation', i.e. the way in which parents encourage or discourage gender appropriate behaviour in children. For example, boys may be discouraged from being emotional whilst boyish behaviour may be tolerated in a female child until adolescence. Lake found that parents differentiate between boys and girls even when they are newborn babies. Mothers tend to be more emotional with female babies and fuss over them more than boys.

Secondly, Oakley identifies 'canalisation', which refers to the way parents channel their children's interests into toys and activities that are gender appropriate. Parents tend to give girls toys which are a preparation for motherhood and domesticity whilst boys' toys offer more scope for excitement and intellectual stimulation.

e Here is an excellent use of a sociological study, i.e. Oakley, supported by research, i.e. Lake, and applied examples.

However, these ideas can be criticised for two reasons. Firstly, ideas about gender role socialisation tend to be a little deterministic. Socialisation is not a one-way process. Evidence suggests that children may negotiate gender role socialisation with their parents, and that the latter may be influenced by their children. Gender role socialisation also ignores the fact that many young women today are not following traditional gender paths. Success in education means that they are following careers in large numbers.

Secondly, the theory of gender role socialisation implies that socialisation into traditional gender roles is negative and that somehow the mother-housewife role is of less status or is less important than having a career. However, Hakim points out that many women choose to become mothers and gain great satisfaction from this role.

This evaluation focuses generally on gender role socialisation rather than the specific points raised by Oakley. However, Oakley's points are part of a wider theory of gender role socialisation and consequently this evaluation is a developed and full assessment. It receives the full 18 marks.

(d) In order to assess whether a variety of feminine and masculine identities have emerged in recent years, we need to identify how femininity and masculinity have been traditionally viewed in the UK. Traditional expectations in regard to gender behaviour have resulted in gender stereotyping in regard to both male and female roles. For example, males have been traditionally seen as breadwinners, heads of households, authoritarian leaders and technical/scientific handymen who rationally, logically, assertively and without emotion, actively organise the social world. Females, on the other hand, have been traditionally portrayed as existing in two parallel gendered universes. The first is the private sphere of the home and family in which women are seen as best suited to the roles of domestic goddess, homemaker, wife, romantic, shopper-consumer, mother and emotional caretaker. The second stereotype views certain types of women as primarily sexual beings. Cultural institutions like the media are engaged in the sexual objectification of women's bodies, reducing them to dizzy blondes, bimbos and a collection of body parts readily available to men.

This section rightly focuses on what came before the newly emerging forms of gender. It shows an intelligent grasp of concepts and uses examples in an applied fashion.

Many sociologists have argued in recent years that these stereotypes are now under sustained attack because of economic and cultural changes that have occurred over the last few decades. In particular, UK society has experienced a feminisation of the labour force and economy. Traditional manual jobs dominated by males have gone into decline, resulting in high rates of male unemployment, whilst the majority of new jobs created have gone to women. Moreover females have also enjoyed unprecedented educational success in recent decades. It is therefore believed that women have acquired both economic and cultural power. They no longer have to be economically dependent upon a male breadwinner.

The candidate provides a full explanation of why there might be newly emerging gender roles which taps into social trends very well.

It is claimed that such economic trends have led to cultural changes. For example, Sharpe found when she repeated her classic research of working-class girls, *Just Like a Girl*, in the mid-1990s that girls no longer saw marriage and children as a priority. Careers and economic independence from men were their main goals.

question

Helen Wilkinson in *Genderquake* argues that young females today are ambitious for careers and are no longer content to follow traditional paths into femininity. In addition, they demand more from men and marriage and are quite happy to use divorce as a means of escape from an unhappy marriage. They are no longer willing to tolerate empty shell marriages, abusive men or men unwilling to share the domestic burden. Chandler notes that such women are opting to live in single-person households whilst they develop their career and independence from men.

This is a sociologically focused paragraph that uses a range of sociological studies in a perceptive and focused way to answer the question.

Men too have been seen to be undergoing fundamental change. Gay men are now more accepted by society whilst media representations of masculinity are increasingly focusing on the feminine side of men by encouraging male consumers to invest time and money on their bodies. Mort argues that the sexualisation of the male body in advertising is becoming a norm.

The essay is balanced by references to masculinity.

Sociologists have argued that the feminisation of the labour force means that men have taken on more emotional caring roles, especially in regard to childcare. There is no doubt that men are more involved, e.g. more men than ever attend the birth of their children. However, it is probably an exaggeration to talk about a 'new man' in touch with his feminine side. Countless studies of the domestic division of labour suggest that women who work still have the lion's share of childcare, housework and the emotional maintenance of the household.

This is an evaluative paragraph which intelligently questions the notion that new masculinities are appearing.

Sociologists such as Mac An Ghaill argue that the feminisation of the economy has led to a crisis in masculinity as traditional men are prevented from carrying out traditional roles such as breadwinning. It is suggested that this has led to problems such as increased suicide among young men. Some men may also feel threatened by women as economic providers and resort to violence as compensation.

Excellent knowledge of sociological studies is demonstrated. If the candidate had the time, references to male underachievement in education could be made.

In conclusion, there is no doubt that there exists a variety of femininities and masculinities today. However, these have not replaced traditional forms and nor have they displaced masculinity as the dominant gender role. Despite progress in the economy, women are still paid 18% less than men, are still denied access to top jobs, and are still mainly responsible for the family. As Delamont argues, the degree of change for most men and women has been minimal.

The candidate provides an evaluative conclusion that demonstrates a perceptive grasp of the key points and focuses on the issues embodied in the essay question.

e Part (d) is a very good example of the types of skill required for success at AS. It consequently scores 14 marks for knowledge and understanding, 4 marks for interpretation and analysis and 8 marks for evaluation, making a full 26 marks.

Overall mark: 60/60

The formation and meaning of ethnic identities

Item A

Modood's survey of ethnic minority groups found that many of his second-generation sample thought of themselves as mostly — but not entirely — having a British identity. However, their experience of racism meant that most people in his sample tended to see their ethnic culture or religion as more important than being British. This was because they believed that the majority of white people did not see them as British. They therefore compensated for this by focusing on other aspects of their identity, e.g. being proud of their skin colour, stressing elements of religious belief, closely abiding by traditional cultural rules etc.

(a) **Identify and briefly explain two ways in which Item A challenges the idea of a unified British identity.** (8 marks)

(b) **Identify and briefly explain two ways in which the values of young members of an ethnic minority might clash with those of their parents.** (8 marks)

(c) **Outline and briefly evaluate two ways in which religion may act as a secondary agent of socialisation.** (18 marks)

(d) **Discuss the view that ethnic minority cultures may use aspects of ethnic identity to resist racism.** (26 marks)

Total: 60 marks

■ ■ ■

Answer to question 3: grade-C candidate

(a) Modood says black people do not feel British.

> *e* This point is too brief, although it does relate directly to the concept of British identity. An explanation was required.

Racism too is a problem for black people.

> *e* It is not clear how this impacts on British identity. The response scores 3 out of a possible 8 marks because it fails to develop explanations.

(b) Asian people may insist that their children go through an arranged marriage against their will. This is a major problem in their communities.

> *e* This is a generalisation that only touches upon a potential conflict.

There may be a clash between older and younger members of an ethnic minority group in relation to dress. For example, young Asian girls might want to follow western fashion but may be forced to wear traditional clothing like headscarves.

e This is a better example, although it is largely anecdotal. It would have picked up more marks if it had been linked to a sociological study. The response scores 4 out of a possible 8 marks.

(c) Religion is very important to some ethnic minority groups. From a very young age, if you are a Pakistani, you will come into frequent contact with religious ideas. You may have to go to the mosque regularly and it is likely that you will have to learn sections of the Koran. Islam shapes a lot of aspects of family life, e.g. respect for parents, attitudes towards marriage etc. Jacobson notes that Islam will affect what you eat, how you behave outside the family and how you see white society.

e This is quite good despite its anecdotal feel. The reference to Jacobson is accurate. It was a good idea to focus on 'Pakistanis' rather than generalising about Asians.

However, it is important to remember that a lot of this will depend on class and gender. For example, middle-class Muslims may be more relaxed about abiding by Islamic rules when compared to people living in deprived areas, whilst girls are more socially controlled than boys.

e This is not a bad evaluation despite its lack of evidence and potential for over-generalisation. It displays conceptual understanding.

A second way in which religion may act as a secondary agent of socialisation is to educate us via Sunday school and school assemblies about Christianity. This is useful because it may provide us with lessons or moral guidelines on how to deal with certain situations. For example, most people in the UK disapprove of adultery, according to surveys. Moral disapproval of adultery is therefore a cultural norm that probably has its roots in the Ten Commandments. However, such religious influence is probably in decline as Sunday school attendance is no longer popular and school assemblies increasingly include no religious content.

e This is a less well-developed 'way', but good points are made about morality. The evaluation focuses well on the way identified. Unfortunately, it does not link to any sociological study. The response to part (c) scores 7 out of 10 marks for knowledge and understanding, 4 out of 4 marks for interpretation and analysis, and 3 out of 4 marks for evaluation, making 14 out of 18.

(d) The view that ethnic minority cultures may use aspects of ethnic identity to resist racism is very true. However, before we look at this, we must define what we mean by 'ethnic minority'. This used to be used to describe black people such as Asians and West Indians who arrived in Britain in the 1950s. In 2001, most ethnic minority people living in the UK were British-born.

e This introduction is only partially successful. The candidate attempts to define terms, which is commendable. A very good point is made about British-born minorities, but terms like 'black', 'white' and 'Asian' are used uncritically.

Racism is a major problem in our society. For example, the Stephen Lawrence inquiry concluded that the police were suffering from institutional racism — they pick on black people, especially West Indians, because they believe them to be criminal. The belief is false. They are no more criminals than white people. Some West Indians have responded to police racism by becoming Rastafarians. This religion believes that white society should not be cooperated with and that God will destroy it one day.

e The candidate makes a good reference to the Stephen Lawrence inquiry. A reasonable conceptual understanding of institutional racism is demonstrated, although the illustration is not very sophisticated. The reference to Rastafarianism is valid, but needed to be supported by a study.

Asian people experience a lot of racism too. For example, some Asian taxi drivers have been killed in racist attacks in recent years, and in Bradford this year, white racists from the National Front caused a riot by marching through an Asian area.

e This is anecdotal evidence, but valid.

Some young Asians have had enough of this treatment and have set up vigilante groups to seek revenge on racists. Other Asian people have turned to Islam for support. Gardner and Shukur point out that young unemployed Pakistanis who believe that white society is racist get great comfort from Islam because it provides them with status and identity denied by white society.

e The first part is too anecdotal now, but the reference to Gardner and Shukur is relevant and well used.

In conclusion, then, ethnic minority culture can be quite useful in defending people from racism. However, sociologists like Johal, Butler etc. argue that young black people prefer to mix socially with their white peers rather than never come into contact with them. Johal found that many young Asians believed in having a hybrid identity where they would take what they regarded as the best from both Asian and white British worlds.

e This is the only evaluation in the whole essay. It is not a bad point, but it is not exactly clear how it relates to racism. More evaluation is necessary to lift this answer into the top band.

e The response to part (d) scores 9 out of 14 marks for knowledge and under-standing. The candidate demonstrates reasonable knowledge of the issue but needed to link racism and aspects of ethnic minority culture more firmly. The essay refers to some studies but is overreliant on anecdotal evidence. The response scores 2 out of 4 marks for interpretation and analysis because it needed to focus more consistently on the question. It is awarded 4 out of 8 marks for evaluation because it lacks evaluative range. The mark for part (d) is therefore 15 out of 26.

Overall mark: 36/60

Task

After reading through the examiner's comments, rewrite part (d) so that:

- your introduction sets the scene for the debate
- you acknowledge the difficulty in using terms such as 'Asian' accurately
- you outline how racism affects ethnic minority group culture using three key sociological studies, e.g. Gardner and Shukur, Modood, Jacobson, Abercrombie and Warde
- you construct three evaluative observations

■ ■ ■

Answer to question 3: grade-A candidate

(a) Modood found that many second-generation members of ethnic minority groups did not see themselves as British because they suspected that the majority of British people did not accept them as British. Such a view probably has some validity when we consider that 30% of the British population admitted to feelings of prejudice towards ethnic minorities in a recent British Social Attitudes survey.

e The candidate successfully identifies a way and explains it clearly. The evidence from the BSA survey is an excellent illustrative link.

In addition, members of ethnic minority groups wanted to feel British but their everyday experience of racism undermined their sense of belonging. For example, evidence suggests that ethnic minority groups frequently experience racist name-calling, violence and institutional racism in the UK today.

e A second way is well identified and different types of racism are offered in explanation. The candidate scores the full 8 marks for clearly interpreting the item and offering explanations fully supported by illustrative data.

(b) Charlotte Butler's research into young Islamic women indicates that they often subscribe to quite different identities from their mothers with regard to equality, domestic roles, fashion and marriage. However, despite these generational conflicts, she does note that these women are committed to Islam.

e Here is a good use of an empirical study to identify and explain aspects of inter-generational conflict.

Song's research into the Chinese in Britain also demonstrates how the values of younger members of an ethnic minority might clash with those of their parents. She researched families who ran take-away businesses in southeast England. She discovered that Chinese children who wanted to gain qualifications and go to university and did not want to follow their parents into the family business were regarded as 'less Chinese' than those who abided by their parents' wishes.

e This demonstrates excellent use of a contemporary empirical study to identify and explain aspects of inter-generational conflict. The candidate scores the full 8 marks.

question

(c) Sociologists like Tischer argue that religion is an important agency of socialisation because it socialises people into moral values. He notes that religion functions to provide people with moral guidelines which will influence all aspects of their behaviour. Other agencies of socialisation, especially education, act as channels for such moral socialisation. For example, our overall experience of moral education means that our behaviour in relation to marriage, family life, abiding by the law, respect for others and blasphemy is often shaped by moral values. We may claim not to be religious but religious morality originating in the Bible, the Ten Commandments etc. underpins most people's behaviour. However, sociologists working from a postmodern perspective are critical of this view and argue that people's behaviour and values are likely to be shaped by a global popular or mass culture which people acquire from frequent contact with the media. In other words, they argue that the media are more important as an agency of socialisation than religion, which is in decline.

> The candidate provides an extensive outline that references both a study and a theory, although the latter is optional at this level. The evaluation focuses on outlining an alternative approach.

Secondly, religion is important in helping shape national identity. National ceremonies and rituals such as royal weddings, Remembrance Sunday, the Coronation etc. aim to celebrate aspects of Britishness. Consequently being British is often equated with religion because Christianity and Christian values often underpin these nationalistic rituals, as seen in the use of the Lord's Prayer, the singing of hymns etc. and the fact that these ceremonies are often supervised by the Archbishop of Canterbury. Some conflict sociologists are critical of this because they argue that we are being socialised into uncritically accepting the traditions of the ruling elite and the hierarchy and inequality that characterised modern societies.

> This makes a good link to national identity, although the evaluation needed to make clearer the link between the values of the ruling elite and religion. Other alternative points of evaluation could have been made, e.g. the candidate could have linked religion to ethnic minority culture. However, the candidate demonstrates a range of knowledge and understanding of two ways in which religion operates as an agency of socialisation, and consequently scores 9 out of 10 marks for this skill. The response addresses the question set and selects appropriate evidence, scoring 4 out of 4 marks for interpretation and analysis. Evaluation is well developed in terms of one way, but needed further clarification in regard to the second way, and the candidate consequently scores 2 out of 4 marks for this skill, making a total of 15 out of 18.

(d) In the UK, ethnicity is often associated by white people with minority groups from the former British colonies of the Indian subcontinent, the Caribbean and Africa. This definition is unsatisfactory because it is based on skin colour rather than common cultural characteristics. As Mason argues, the white British tend to see ethnicity as something other groups have. They consequently may view ethnic minorities with suspicion and construct stereotypical and racist assumptions about them (i.e. prejudice) and may even practise racial discrimination. For example, the McPherson Report recently argued that the London Metropolitan police are institutionally racist.

e Here is a good introduction that focuses on (a) how we define the problematical nature of ethnicity and (b) how this affects the way that the majority culture interacts with ethnic minority cultures. The references to Mason and McPherson demonstrate that conceptual confidence is particularly developed.

This prejudice and discrimination has an effect upon the ethnic minority culture and how it interacts with the majority culture. For example, Modood argues that ethnic minority people may be less willing to identify with being British if they feel that the British public do not want them moving in next door. The reaction might be that ethnic minority people take refuge from such racism by throwing themselves into celebrating aspects of their subculture, e.g. religion, traditions and rituals, family life etc.

e This focuses on the central question, i.e. how ethnic minorities react to racism in terms of their culture. The reference to Modood is a good use of the item.

This especially seems the case with young people. Evidence from Troyna and Mac An Ghaill suggests that some African-Caribbean youth form anti-school subcultures based on Rasta culture. They deliberately flout school rules by growing dreadlocks and talk in Creole patois so that teachers cannot understand them.

e The candidate uses educational studies in a focused fashion to illustrate potential cultural responses.

Other studies focus on how some Asian youth, especially Pakistanis and Bangladeshis, are turning to Islam as a means of resisting racism. Jacobson found that young Pakistanis saw being Muslim as more important than being either British or Pakistani. As a result, Islam had a profound impact on their personal identity and affected all aspects of their lives in terms of diet, dress, education, worship and everyday practices. Castells suggests Islam appeals to young unemployed Pakistanis because it stresses the 'exclusion of the excluders' (i.e. racist whites) by the excluded (i.e. Pakistanis). Abercrombie and Warde argue that young African-Caribbeans use black history and music, especially hip-hop, rap and reggae, as a means of coping with and resisting what they see as white oppression.

e This is an excellent section that demonstrates a perceptive understanding of the issues embodied in the question. A range of empirical studies are used which display perceptive knowledge of issues and evidence.

However, to conclude, it is important not to exaggerate these processes. Racism is a real problem but many members of ethnic minority groups do not react in these defensive ways. For example, Johal's work indicates that many second-

generation Asians regard themselves as having a dual identity in that they see themselves as both Asian and British. Johal notes that such a dual or hybrid identity results in them switching cultural identities depending on whether they are with their families or white peers. Such switching allows them to make the best of both worlds and suggests a positive future in terms of the relationship between ethnic minority culture and white culture. The evidence in terms of African-Caribbean culture is also positive in that statistics indicate that 50% of African-Caribbean men have a white partner.

e Here is a developed evaluation using Johal's work, but the candidate does not make the most of the point about African-Caribbean culture. A couple of more evaluative points could have been added from the following list: there are signs that racism is now being taken seriously and tackled by the authorities; cultural awareness and defensive reactions may be the result of tensions between ethnic minority groups in some areas; the attitudes of the second and third generation may be shaped by inter-generational conflict; and racism is not a homogeneous or universal experience.

e Despite being a little on the brief side, this is a sophisticated and focused response that addresses part (d) throughout. It demonstrates conceptual confidence and an excellent understanding of the need to link evidence to particular strands of the debate. Evaluation, however, required further development. The answer therefore scores 13 out of 14 marks for knowledge and understanding, 4 out of 4 marks for interpretation and analysis, and 4 out of 8 marks for evaluation, making a total of 21 out of 26.

Overall mark: 52/60

The formation and meaning of national identities

Item A

National identities are shaped by symbols. The flag is one of the most important symbols used by people to identify with groups that share a geographical location, history and culture. For example, the Union Jack, depending on who you are, might symbolise the British Empire, Britishness, the queen, Britpop or right-wing extremist parties like the National Front. The flag may be waved by those groups which feel that their Britishness is being threatened by the external threats, e.g. the euro.

Adapted from Woodward, K. (2000) *Questioning Identity*, Routledge, p. 134.

(a) Using Item A only, identify and briefly explain two ways in which the Union Jack might symbolise national identity in the contemporary UK. (8 marks)
(b) Identify and briefly explain two characteristics of globalisation. (8 marks)
(c) Outline and briefly evaluate two ways in which the education system socialises people into a national identity. (18 marks)
(d) Discuss the view that British national identity is in decline. (26 marks)

Total: 60 marks

Answer to question 4: grade-A candidate

(a) Some people might see the Union Jack as symbolising Britishness because it incorporates the three flags of the home countries: England, Wales and Scotland. Both the Union Jack and the flags of the home countries fly together, for example, outside the Scottish parliament building in Edinburgh. This symbolises that Scotland and the Scottish people are still committed to being part of the UK and see themselves as British as well as Scottish.

e This is a good example that is well explained and illustrated.

In Northern Ireland, the Union Jack has come to symbolise and represent the Protestant or Unionist part of the population that wants to remain part of the UK and which feels threatened by power-sharing with the Republican Irish-Catholic population. The flag in this case is a symbol of resistance and a means of marking out sectarian territory.

e Here is a perceptive way of identifying the importance of the Union Jack, which is well explained. Responses do not have to be this sophisticated. For example, the candidate could have focused on the importance of the flag in sporting events, in

war, as a means of claiming territory, as a symbol of extreme nationalism etc. This candidate scores the full **8 marks** available.

(b) One characteristic of globalisation is that increasingly cultural products such as films and music are produced for the global market. There are fears that this is creating a mass entertainment culture which is undermining national and ethnic identities.

e The candidate identifies a feature of globalisation, but the explanation needs a little bit more detail, e.g. how the mass culture might be affecting identity. An example would help.

Another characteristic of globalisation is the increasing diversity and choice found in the market place. According to some sociologists, this has resulted in people putting more emphasis on consumption of global brands and logos. Young people, in particular, are seen to have their identity shaped by such global market forces. Klein, for example, suggests that young people's identity and personal space are exploited by global corporations and brands.

e This is an excellent example of identification and explanation. It clearly identifies a characteristic and explains it in full with a specific example. The candidate scores **7 out of a possible 8 marks**.

(c) The curriculum of most schools in the UK openly teaches British history, language and literature. In many Welsh schools, the curriculum is taught in Welsh. These processes obviously socialise pupils into a national identity and promote a sense of belonging to a common national culture. However, the academic curriculum of schools in the UK has been criticised for being ethno-centric. The UK is now a multicultural society, yet the curriculum overwhelm-ingly focuses on a white, Christian and British view of the world. For example, the teaching of British history focuses on white achievements in terms of empire, and black people may be portrayed negatively. This may discourage feelings of being British.

e The candidate focuses on outlining how the academic or formal curriculum socialises pupils, and the example of Wales is used where the process is more obvious. The evaluation is perceptive and rightly focused on the multicultural nature of British society.

Some sociologists note the existence of a hidden curriculum which contributes to national identity. This socialises people in subtle and unconscious ways into conforming to a national identity. Some sociologists are critical of the content of history specifications in the UK because they tend to focus on traditional 'kings and queens' type history, which generally celebrates the achievements of elites rather than ordinary people, and conquest, war and domination of world trade. Critical sociologists argue that such knowledge encourages acceptance of hierarchy, patriarchy, class inequality, racism and white dominance. Nationalistic values from this perspective are essentially the values of the ruling class.

📝 An excellent outline is provided and the evaluation is both clear and sociologically focused. The only real concern here is a lack of reference to sociological studies, but in some areas of The Individual and Society, these are few and far between and, in this case, the conceptual confidence of the candidate compensates for this. It is important to understand that there are no perfect or ideal answers to questions set by examiners. If candidates do all that is demanded of them by the mark scheme, they should be rewarded full marks. This is a response that fits into that category. The candidate therefore scores 10 marks for knowledge and understanding, 4 for interpretation and analysis, and 4 for evaluation, gaining the full 18 marks.

(d) Before we can discuss whether British identity is in decline, we have to consider what we mean by 'national identity'. This generally refers to the feeling of being part of a larger community, i.e. a nation. This gives people a sense of purpose, meaning and belonging. Usually a national identity results from socialisation into a common national culture. Education, mass media and sport in particular reinforce our sense of national identity. For example, during the World Cup supporters express their national identity by painting their faces in their national colours and flags. National identity therefore promotes nationalism — that is, strong beliefs in the superiority of your nation, symbolic behaviour such as flag waving, and fervent patriotism.

📝 The candidate sets out a considered introduction that rightly sees the need to define the terms and concepts used in the essay. All part (d) responses are mini-essays, so an introduction along these lines is always recommended. This candidate demonstrates an excellent understanding of concepts and uses a good example, i.e. the World Cup, to illustrate.

When we think of British identity, a number of symbols, institutions, images and ideas instantly come to mind, e.g. the monarchy, Parliament, the Union Jack, John Bull, drinking tea, fish and chips, roast beef and Yorkshire pudding, the weather etc. We think of these things as uniquely British. There are negative things that we think are uniquely British too, e.g. football hooliganism.

📝 The candidate sees the need to move on to British identity. The examples used are well considered and focused on British identity. The reference to negative symbols of Britishness is particularly good.

Schudsen points out that we think of these things as British because we have been socialised into a common British culture through the common use of the English language, the teaching of British history and literature and the emphasis on Christian worship in schools. National rituals, e.g. the celebration of Easter and Christmas and national ceremonies such as the Coronation, strongly imply that Britishness and Christianity are one and the same. Symbols such as the Union Jack, the national anthem and passports also encourage a feeling of being British, e.g. the Welsh, Scots and Irish are issued with British passports, not Celtic ones. The mass media encourage us to identify with symbols

of Britishness such as the royal family and to be proud of such British products as the Rolls-Royce and the Spice Girls. Even Tony Blair has talked of a 'Cool Britannia'.

> An appropriate study, i.e. Schudsen, is referenced, but what is particularly impressive is the grasp of the concept of socialisation and the range of examples used to illustrate aspects of it. This is an excellent example of the applied sociology we want to reward at AS. Be aware that the range of examples used is very wide — two or three would have been sufficient, if focused, to illustrate the socialisation process.

However, sociologists such as Anderson suggest that British identity is based on myth rather than reality. He argues that most of the rituals, institutions and ceremonies associated with Britishness are recent inventions, e.g. the royal family only became popular with the general public in the latter half of the twentieth century. According to Anderson, many symbols of being British were deliberately invented to bring together the very different ethnic groups of English, Scots, Welsh and Irish in order to ensure social order.

> The candidate uses a sociological study, i.e. Anderson, to evaluate the notion of British identity and points out, using focused examples, that it is a social invention. This paragraph is a good example of a candidate focusing on the key command word 'discuss'.

Three recent social developments and trends have threatened the stability of British identity and have led to the view that British identity is in decline. Firstly, the rise of Celtic nationalism has led to political power being given back to Scotland, Wales and Northern Ireland. The existence of Celtic identity has always undermined the view that a British identity exists. For example, the Welsh have always strongly emphasised the Welsh language and have their own Welsh-speaking television channels whilst Scotland has an educational and legal system which is very different from the rest of Britain. There has never been a strong enthusiasm for British sports teams, especially a British football team.

> Contemporary and convincing examples are used to illustrate the point that British identity has always been a problematical concept.

Secondly, British identity becomes a problem when we consider the multicultural nature of British society today. Modood points out that many black Britons may be reluctant to see themselves as British first because they think white Britons do not fully accept them. There is evidence that young members of ethnic minority groups reject Britishness because of racism. Jacobson found that young Pakistanis saw themselves as Muslim first and foremost.

> The candidate develops the argument further by dipping into revision notes on ethnic identity. You should be aware that national and ethnic identities are often interlinked.

Thirdly, British identity may be undermined by international pressures such as those coming from the European Union. For example, in recent years, the pound has become a powerful symbol of Britishness as people feel threatened by European power and especially the euro. The globalisation of culture through films, music and advertising brands has also been seen as responsible for 'diluting' symbols of British culture. For example, Hollywood has been criticised for Americanising Shakespeare, Winnie the Pooh etc.

e The candidate is aware of contemporary events and touches upon postmodernist arguments. Remember that at this level a detailed theoretical outline is not required.

In conclusion, the idea that British identity is in decline really depends on whether you believe that it had a strong existence in the first place. Sociologists suggest that generally British identity was never strong and was always under pressure from Scottish, Welsh and Irish demands to retain their own very distinctive identities. Other modern pressures, such as those from Europe and those caused by globalisation of popular culture, have weakened traditional ideas about Britishness and perhaps given rise to problems such as racism, especially among the English who have never enjoyed the distinctive sense of identity enjoyed by the Scots etc. Finally, some have argued that a new form of Britishness is appearing in the fields of media, food, fashion and music as the diverse groups, black, Asian and whites, that make up the people inhabiting the United Kingdom interact, intermarry and share their cultural experiences.

e This is a very focused, evaluative conclusion. Many essays do not include such conclusions. We recommend them because they allow you to focus on the issues included in the essay title and to address the question directly. This candidate recaps some of the arguments raised in the essay. If you don't have time for this, do try and conclude by focusing and developing a point related to what has gone before, but which you have not yet raised in detail. The final point made above is an excellent example of this.

e We could not ask for a better essay than this from an AS student and it consequently scores the full 14 marks for knowledge and understanding, 4 marks for interpretation and analysis, and 8 marks for evaluation, making 26 in all.

Overall mark: 59/60

The formation and meaning of class identities (II)

Item A

Social class can provide us with a sense of belonging and a strongly developed sense of class identity. For example, Frank Parkin noted that some manual workers, especially those employed in traditional industries such as coal-mining, subscribe to a 'proletarian traditionalist' working-class culture and identity. Such workers value community and mutual support, which is reflected in their commitment to extended family relationships and organisations such as trade unions and working men's clubs. They also see capitalist society as sharply divided by social class inequalities. They consequently have a strong sense of injustice and see the world as characterised by conflict between 'us' and 'them' (i.e. the rich).

(a) **Using Item A, identify and briefly explain two values associated with working-class identity.** (8 marks)

(b) **Identify and briefly explain two cultural norms associated with the underclass.** (8 marks)

(c) **Outline and briefly evaluate two ways in which middle-class identity might be shaped by the workplace.** (18 marks)

(d) **Discuss the view that the middle classes in the contemporary UK have a strongly developed sense of class culture and identity.** (26 marks)

Total: 60 marks

■ ■ ■

Answer to question 5: grade-A candidate

(a) Firstly, traditional working-class identity or proletarian traditionalists value the concept of community. Community is especially strong in dangerous working-class jobs because it is important that workers are strongly supportive of each other. Such community is carried over into working men's clubs and into the organisation of family life. There is evidence that working-class family members feel a strong sense of obligation to each other.

    The candidate successfully identifies 'community' as an important value from the item and develops a detailed and sociologically focused illustration of the concept.

Secondly, such workers probably have a strongly developed sense of political identity in that they are likely to subscribe to a strong sense of class awareness and injustice. This may be reinforced and encouraged by common membership of trade unions and collective action. The feeling that they have little in common with employers or white-collar workers, i.e. 'them versus us', probably increases working-class community.

e The candidate links the point about 'them' and 'us' in the item to the concept of political identity in an intelligent fashion. Overall, then, this is a strong response that makes the most of the information in the item and uses strong examples to support the explanations. It scores the full **8 marks**.

(b) Some sociologists argue that the underclass subscribe to norms of behaviour which are essentially immoral and deviant. For example, Murray suggests that members of the underclass do not follow conventional norms when it comes to marriage and child-rearing. It is suggested that the underclass is promiscuous in terms of its sexual behaviour, that males are not committed to long-term relationships, especially when children are involved, and single mothers are ineffective in bringing up their children, who are consequently involved in a career of crime.

e The candidate identifies a relevant norm of behaviour, i.e. immorality, and clearly explains, using focused examples, why the behaviour of the underclass may be defined as a social problem.

Secondly, it is also argued that the underclass is not committed to work. Its members allegedly are not interested in holding down full-time jobs and are instead feckless and idle. They are supposedly more interested in living off the state, i.e. welfare dependency. However, surveys of those living in poverty in the UK have found very little evidence that the so-called underclass subscribe to these values and norms.

e Here is another excellent point that is well illustrated. The candidate offers an evaluative point, but this was not required by the question. The candidate again scores the full **8 marks**.

(c) The values of professionals such as doctors and lawyers are often shaped by the workplace in the shape of the professional associations to which they belong. These often produce ethical and professional codes which act as moral guidelines for the behaviour of such occupations. For example, both the medical and legal profession are bound by rules of confidentiality and members can be 'struck off' if they are found guilty of professional malpractice and negligence. Professionals often use these rules to suggest that they have a higher calling than other occupations and therefore deserve their higher status and rewards. However, some critical sociologists suggest that professionals have too much power and are not accountable enough to the public they serve. This may result in abuses of occupational trust and power as in the Harold Shipman case.

e This candidate focuses on the workplace culture of professional workers in a clear and convincing fashion. The evaluative point is perceptive.

White-collar workers may have a confused sense of middle-class identity because of the nature of their workplace. In recent years, white-collar work has undergone

question

a revolution in terms of its organisation. In particular, Braverman argues that computerisation and the deskilling that tends to accompany it have transformed white-collar work from a skilled craft into a routinised, low-skilled and low-paid occupation. Consequently the job has lost social status. For example, Mackintosh and Mooney note how the culture of call centres is characterised by control of workers through surveillance. Rising discontent and unionisation may be evidence of a growing consciousness among white-collar workers of being working class. Braverman calls this proletarianisation. However, some sociologists are sceptical of this. They point out that such workers are likely to have instrumental identities in that they compete with each other for promotion and performance-related pay. In other words, the workplace encourages the pursuit of individual rather than collective interests.

> This is a rather full outline that concentrates on workplace changes in regard to white-collar workers and uses studies and concepts in a focused fashion. The candidate successfully evaluates by focusing on an alternative account of the culture of white-collar workers. This candidate therefore scores the full 18 marks for this section.

(d) Abercrombie and Warde (2000) note that since 1945 the UK has experienced an impressive growth in the number of people employed in middle-class non-manual jobs. Many sociologists today prefer to use the term 'the middle classes' because they argue that non-manual work is characterised by distinct social groups or class fractions which differ from each other in terms of economic rewards and assets, lifestyle and cultural attitudes.

> The candidate gives a good introduction that sets out some relevant facts about the growth of middle-class jobs and attempts to define why sociologists use the concept of 'middle classes' rather than 'middle class'.

However, Alison Light argues that these middle-class fractions do share three broad characteristics. Firstly, they subscribe to a middle-class identity based on home ownership and commuting from the suburbs. Secondly, suburban middle-class culture suffers from a social anxiety about being seen to do the right thing. In practice, this means communicating social position to others. For example, this may be done through conspicuous consumption (i.e. buying luxury items in order to acquire status), 'proper' use of language and having the 'right' accent. The home and the garden, in particular, symbolise social aspiration. Thirdly, the suburban lifestyle is essentially traditional and conservative in thought and action. Sudden change is not welcomed but seen as dangerous and threatening. The suburban mindset sees society in moral decline and consequently change must be resisted. Respectability, decency and self-control are seen as central to middle-class life.

> This is an excellent section which uses the work of Light in a manner that directly addresses the question. The candidate clearly has conceptual confidence and applies examples well.

There is some evidence that this suburban middle-class identity may be fragmenting. For example, Savage (1995) argues that there are differences between the professional middle class and the managerial middle class. The former have probably succeeded because of cultural capital whilst managers have tended to be upwardly mobile from the working-class shop-floor. Savage argues that these differences influence the lifestyle of these groups. For example, professional leisure time may be spent in cultural pursuits such as visiting museums and art galleries or going to classical concerts. Managerial leisure pursuits are likely to focus on sport.

e This paragraph is a good example of elaborating on the discussion. This part of the essay develops some of the ideas contained in the introduction and references a well-known study in this area.

Savage suggests that differences between these two groups are likely to become more pronounced because managers are experiencing downsizing and redundancy due to mergers, takeovers and falling profits, especially in banking and manufacturing. Professionals, on the other hand, have been able to defend their existing privileges through strong professional associations.

e The candidate displays an excellent understanding of Savage and is thinking through future developments with regard to these groups.

A great deal of attention has been paid to white-collar workers in recent years. Harry Braverman has suggested that clerical work has been subjected to deskilling and consequently white-collar workers no longer enjoy economic advantages over manual workers. It is suggested that a process of proletarianisation has occurred and that this has undermined the middle-class identity of white-collar workers in that the cultural outlook of such workers now resembles that of the working class.

The evidence for this argument is actually mixed. Research by Marshall found that 50% of his white-collar sample saw themselves as working class. However, he also found crucial differences in lifestyle and cultural characteristics between white-collar workers and manual workers. The white-collar sample was much more individualistic in outlook, was less likely to belong to a trade union and more likely to vote Conservative. Furthermore, Marshall's white-collar sample had few working-class friends and spent their money in quite different ways.

e This is another excellent section demonstrating a perceptive knowledge and understanding of the debate about another group traditionally seen as middle class. The candidate displays good interpretation and analysis skills in the choice of studies and application of evidence, and also sees the need to evaluate the argument.

Finally, there is evidence that the self-employed, who have been considered one of the most conservative and individualistic of middle-class groups in terms of beliefs and action, may be becoming more organised and radicalised. There is evidence, although it is mainly anecdotal, from the petrol blockades of 2000 and the foot and mouth crisis of 2001 that self-employed groups such as hauliers and farmers are more willing to take direct action in order to protect their interests.

e Good use of contemporary events is demonstrated here.

Despite the differences identified in this essay, we can see that the one central value that unites all these groups as members of a middle class is their sense of social difference. Much of the cultural behaviour of the middle class can be seen to stem from a shared cultural consciousness that other social groups may be benefiting at their expense.

e This is a fine example of an evaluative conclusion that draws some of the key arguments made in the body of the essay together and concludes with something slightly different from what has gone before.

e This candidate demonstrates a keen and detailed knowledge and understanding of this subject and scores **14** out of **14** for this skill. Full marks are also awarded for both interpretation and analysis, and evaluation, making a total of **26** marks.

Overall mark: 60/60

The formation and meaning of gender identities (II)

Item A

Motherhood as a source of identity appears fixed, stable and rooted in natural biology. Having babies and bringing them up is seen primarily as a biological act because it is based on the woman's natural ability to reproduce. However, Woodward argues that motherhood is not as natural as we think. It is the product of our culture and very much a social construction. Our ideas about motherhood are specific to our society, its culture and its socialisation processes. For example, so-called 'natural' ideas that motherhood should involve women rather than men taking prime responsibility for childcare, that working mothers may 'damage' their children and that there are 'good' and 'bad' mothers are products of culture rather than biology. Other cultures define and treat motherhood very differently. Woodward notes that in our society, a woman is mainly defined on the basis of whom she looks after rather than as an individual with her own distinct personality.

Adapted from Kidd, W. (2000) *Culture and Identity*, Palgrave, p. 180.

(a) **Using Item A, identify and explain two characteristics of women's identity as mothers.** (8 marks)
(b) **Identify and briefly explain two types of masculine identity that exist in the contemporary UK.** (8 marks)
(c) **Outline and briefly evaluate two ways in which occupation may shape female identity.** (18 marks)
(d) **Discuss the view that traditional male identity in the contemporary UK is changing because of a crisis in masculinity.** (26 marks)

Total: 60 marks

■ ■ ■

Task

This question is for you to try yourself. You should spend some time researching suitable material and making notes, and then try to write the answer in 60 minutes — the time you will be allowed in the examination. Below are a few pointers in order to help you get on the right track.

(a) You need to demonstrate interpretation skills in answering this question. The item actually identifies three characteristics associated with the identity of 'mother'. You only have to identify two of them. However, remember that you need to explain what they mean too.

(b) Two types of masculine identity are asked for. Your response could focus on identifying and explaining two exclusively traditional types of masculinity or could explore new types that have emerged in recent years.

(c) Note that occupation usually refers to work and workplace. You need to think very carefully about how going to work for a wage or salary might influence female identity. However, don't ignore housework — it too is an occupation and you might like to explore the effect of being housebound on women's identity. Whatever you decide, you will need to think about how you can criticise or evaluate the two ways you have outlined. You might, for example, focus on how patriarchal influences such as unequal pay, limited access to top jobs, the dual burden of having a full-time job and taking the major responsibility for childcare and housework or the 'crisis in masculinity' negatively impact on women's identity.

(d) Don't forget that this is an essay question and therefore should be organised as one:

- Your introduction should 'set the scene' — that is, clearly but briefly introduce the key arguments and sociologists who have a vested interest in the 'view' contained in the essay title. This will include those who argue for the view as well as those who stand against it. The introduction for this essay might therefore focus on:
  - the traditional view of masculinity. You might link this to those sociologists who believe that gender roles are natural and inevitable, e.g. Norman Dennis, and that, if the roles are changed, this may create social problems
  - defining what is meant by 'the crisis in masculinity', possibly linking to the work of Mac An Ghaill
- Using the work of Mac An Ghaill as your basis, you need to develop the concept of a crisis in masculinity and show how it might have affected masculinity. The following points are worth elaborating and illustrating with reference to trends and sociological studies:
  - the decline of traditional manual jobs in manufacturing and the primary sector of the economy
  - the impact of the increasing feminisation of labour on the male breadwinner role
  - how the increasing economic independence of women may impact on women's attitudes towards marriage and divorce, and therefore on the male's role as head of household
  - the impact on social problems such as male suicide and domestic violence
  - the new man/complicit masculinity
  - the impact on working-class youth identity and attitude towards schooling
  - the impact on juvenile delinquency and urban unrest, e.g. Bea Campbell

You do not have to include all the options listed above in your essay, but those you do include should be supported whenever possible with empirical evidence in the form of sociological studies. Moreover, don't forget to evaluate. For example, the hard empirical evidence in favour of a crisis in masculinity is lacking — especially survey or interview evidence stating how working-class men actually feel. Some sociologists argue that if such a crisis does exist, all it has done is to reaffirm traditional attitudes through behaviour, because men exaggerate their masculinity via crimes such as domestic violence in order to compensate for not being allowed to perform their traditional roles. Sociologists like Dennis, therefore, suggest that if society denies men the opportunity to perform their natural roles, then social problems will result. Finally, feminists like Delamont question how much women's roles and identities have changed in reaction to the crisis in masculinity.